Angels
for everyday living

Angels

for everyday living

Jacky Newcomb

Bounty
Books

An Hachette UK Company
www.hachette.co.uk

This edition published in 2015 by Bounty Books,
a division of Octopus Publishing Group Ltd
Carmelite House
50 Victoria Embankment
London, EC4Y 0DZ
www.octopusbooks.co.uk

ISBN: 978-0-7537-2973-1

A CIP catalogue record for this book is available
from the British Library

Printed and bound in China

10 9 8 7 6 5 4 3 2 1

CONTENTS

INTRODUCTION

Welcome to my exciting new book about connecting with your guardian angels, and thank you so much for choosing it. Together we are going to go on a journey of angelic discovery. I've been researching angelic phenomena for many years now. I originally began my investigation after recalling a childhood angel experience. Let me tell you about it.

Aged five, I got into difficulties while swimming in the sea and angels helped me back to shore. Even though I never saw my angels with my physical eyes, I heard them and felt their loving energy, and that moment changed my life forever. Desperate for information on paranormal subjects, I began reading everything I could get my hands on, and as the internet began to grow I spent hours searching the web. We were the first family we knew with a home computer and certainly the first with an internet connection.

As well as angels, I researched afterlife communication, near-death experiences, out-of-body experiences, life between lives, past lives, and more. It always amazes me how everything is connected, and of course the more information I learn the more I am able to help others. It helped me to work out how everything was pieced together.

Over time, I've learnt more about the different ways in which we can draw closer to the angelic race. Our angels long to work with us, and many people I've met along the way have discovered tricks and tips that made these encounters easier and more fun. I've shared all the best ones with you here, including many I have discovered for myself. I'm sure that you too will find many more ways of reaching out to your angel friends.

Angels have made my life more magical and safe, and less lonely. I've even been 'rescued' several times, especially in the car when voices from another dimension whisper helpful warnings at appropriate times. My angel journey has taken me from talking on TV shows to teaching grief counsellors about angel and afterlife phenomena. I've worked with doctors and nurses, schoolchildren and celebrities. Everyone seems to be interested in angels these days.

HOW THIS BOOK WORKS

I have gathered together lots of fun ways for you to get a little closer to your own guardian angels. The book is split into numerous small sections, so that you can either read it right through from start to finish or dip in pretty well anywhere you want to. You can enjoy the book alone or share sections with friends, working through some of the exercises together. If you prefer, you can read through the text and true-life stories first and then work on the 'angel secrets' and exercises a little at a time; there are no rules, so just do it your way. I suggest you keep a notebook in which to record your angel journey. Write down your thoughts, ideas and experiences as you go along.

True-life stories

I always enjoy reading about real-life angelic encounters. This book is full of angel stories so that you can understand better how angels work with us. Each story is perfect and real, taken from my personal postbag. Real-life angel experiences can be inspirational. Many normal people have occasional angel encounters, but for most of us the angels don't appear in such dramatic ways as they do in these stories. Watch out for more subtle signs in your own life and know that, when the need is at its greatest, the angels will be there in whatever way they can.

Angel secrets

I have loved collecting angel tips and tricks for you to read as you progress through the book. My knowledge has appeared after many years of experience, but I don't mind showing you a few short cuts. Have a go at following the secrets that excite you the most, and have fun with them.

Affirmations

An affirmation is a positive declaration. It can be something you say or something you read. You can create a poster with words on it or a card that you carry around, or just add the words to your computer screensaver. Throughout this book I will give you suggestions for ways of using this powerful tool to work with your own angels and guides.

Exercises

As a girl, I always enjoyed the after-school clubs where we made things and played games – flower club, art club, and many others. 'Play time' is relaxing and it's good for your health. Do you need a better reason? As adults, we don't give ourselves enough time to play, so with this book I give you that permission, and the angels love working with you in this way. 'Imagination' is the key to opening the door to the higher realms. These exercises include things to make, things to do, and quiet-time activities such as meditations.

BRINGING THE ANGELS INTO YOUR LIFE

I hope this book will inspire you to bring the angels into your own life. Your angels are always around you, and if you want to feel that connection you simply need to give them a little time and space, and watch out for those subtle signs. Include these majestic beings in everything you do. Ask them to help and inspire you, ask them to protect and watch over you, and ask them to watch over your loved ones. There are angels for every task and role.

Remember that angels simply want to help you to help yourself rather than take over your life and sort everything out for you. Angels want to empower you so that you can sort out your own problems, and your soul will learn and grow as a result. In the eyes of God, everything that happens in life is seen as an 'experience' (rather than specifically good or bad). Work with love and you will be on the right path.

The suggestions in this book are just that: thoughts and ideas to get you started on your angelic journey. I want to inspire you to come up with your own ideas for angel rituals and fun and, while you're at it, inspire others around you. Be an angel ambassador. Be the magical person you were born to be. Create your own magical places, perform your own angel ceremonies, and share your experiences with others.

Angel blessings.

MEETING ANGELS

'Make yourself familiar with the angels and behold them frequently in spirit; for without being seen, they are present with you.'

St Francis de Sales

There are many different types of angel, but we are most familiar with the angels who watch over humankind – guardian angels. We all have our own guardian angels. They are ever present, ever watchful and always looking out for us.

WHAT DO THEY LOOK LIKE?

Angels number many hundreds of thousands. They are all around us, although most people don't see them. Angels exist on a higher vibration level than humankind. Like the blades on a fan, our eyes can't perceive them most of the time, yet they are there just the same.

They are genderless but often appear as male to show strength and power, or female to show gentleness and compassion. They appear to us in a way that is easy for us to understand, which means human-like in appearance but usually much taller, glowing, white, and with wings and a halo of light surrounding them. Although you would imagine that being in their presence would make you extremely fearful, they seem to be able to surround us with a feeling of great happiness, peace and bliss. An encounter with an angel is a very memorable experience indeed!

Angels are thought to have existed since the beginning of time. Although most people can't see them, there seems no shortage of people who have had encounters with them. Angels interact with us whenever and wherever they can; certainly many see them when they are in danger or are unwell.

WHAT IS A GUARDIAN ANGEL?

We each have angels assigned to us from birth. Our angel has knowledge of our hopes and dreams, goals and achievements. Our angels watch over us, help to keep us out of danger and guide us, keeping us to the path that best suits the learning and growth of the soul. Sometimes our path is easy and at other times it is harder. This is when we usually grow the most.

Traditionally, angels were seen as beings of light and almost all religions have these 'light beings' incorporated into their belief system. Their roles are many and varied, but include looking after planets, bodies of water, plants and flowers, animals, birds and fish, not to mention the movement of the stars in the Universe.

HOW CAN I SEE MY ANGELS?

Our brains find it easier to accept the appearance of our angels and guides when we are in a meditative state or light trance, or perhaps during dream-state visitation (when our bodies are asleep but our minds are awake and aware, also known as 'lucid dreaming'). Not only is it easier for us to acknowledge these great beings of light at this time, but it is also easier for them to appear to us while we are in an altered state of consciousness. Sometimes people even see angels when they are unconscious or during an operation or near-death experience – again, in states of consciousness outside our normal waking awareness. That means, of course, that we can 'create' situations where the angels can appear to us as physical-looking beings, not by putting ourselves in danger but by meditating and inviting them to appear to us, or asking them to visit us when we dream at night.

Angels exist on a different vibration to humankind. Like water, which becomes a gas at higher temperatures and a solid at lower ones, angels are finer in substance than humans are in their earthly bodies. Our limited human vision means we can't see them easily, but remember our lack of ability to see them doesn't mean they don't exist. Angels are as real as you and I.

Throughout this book, I want to offer you many suggestions of ways in which you can interact with your angels, including fun activities and simple exercises, such as making an angel manifestation poster or divination cards. Some will appeal to you more than others (depending on your interests). Start with those that excite you, and most of all have fun.

You can't do something wrong – work with love and you work with the angels. Follow your angel instinct; listen to your inner feelings which will guide you to the best way forward in every situation. Trust your instincts – it's your angel calling.

EXERCISE: Ask an angel to visit while you sleep

If you believe in praying, take the opportunity to talk to your angels when you say your prayers at night. Although people don't pray to angels directly, God will send his messengers to those who need his help. It is OK to ask angels (or God) to help others in need too, and this is the best time to do so.

1 Just before you go to bed, ask your angels to appear to you in a dream. If you're lucky, you will get a sign that they have received your request. Some people receive messages in dreams as symbols and others hear actual words as their sign. Maybe you will be lucky enough to see an angel directly, or your very own guardian angel may appear before you. When you are on the very edge of sleep, just as you fall asleep or immediately before you wake up, this is the time when angels are most likely to bring you a message or sign. Of course, if the angels bring your sign just as you wake up, you are more likely to remember your special visit.

2 Write your experience down. This acts as both a reminder and an encouragement for your angels to communicate with you in this way again. Whenever it is possible, share your experiences with others who are interested. Your angel experiences are meant to be shared. Spread the word.

HOW CAN I MEET MY GUARDIAN ANGEL?

Guardian angels are a feature of many religions but you don't have to be religious to believe in angels; nor do you even need to believe in angels to have a guardian angel. Our angels are with us whether we believe in their existence or not.

Most people want to meet their guardian angels – it is quite normal to be inquisitive. As humans it is easier for us to create a relationship with a being that we have seen 'visually' or communicate with on a regular basis.

By taking time for regular meditation, you can build up this relationship with your guardian angel in the same way that you might with a long-standing friend. Your angel has been your friend for eternity and now it is time to reacquaint yourself with your special guide and guardian.

Here are some things you might want from your guardian angel:

- Their name

- Something about their personality or what they might look like

- Information about their role in your life and how specifically your angel can help you in day-to-day living

- Answers to difficult questions and problems

- Direction and guidance

- Information about your future

- Insight into personal relationships

- Assistance with money

- Health and healing

- Spiritual guidance

- Assistance with family, particularly watching over children

- Help with grief

- Support with job changes and careers

- Help with studying

- Guidance on how you might manifest your dreams

ANGEL SECRET

Your angel is always with you, longing to give you a subtle sign that they are close by. Ask your angel to bring you a white feather as a gift from the heavenly realms. White feathers have long been said to be the calling card of the angels.

EXERCISE: Meet your guardian angel – Meditation 1

Your meditation begins with a simple relaxation exercise (steps 1–8 below). You can use this exercise for any meditations you create for yourself later on.

Start by instructing each part of your body in turn to relax. When you feel relaxed and receptive, then your journey can begin. Use background music if you wish. If at any time you feel uncomfortable, just open your eyes and then go and make yourself a hot drink until you feel 'grounded' and back in the moment once more.

1 Make sure you are comfortable. Find a warm room in which you won't be disturbed for at least one hour and unplug or switch off any telephones, TVs and radios.

2 Sit in an upright chair if you can, keeping your back fairly straight, and placing your feet on the ground (or on a cushion on the floor).

3 Take a deep, cleansing breath in through your nose, hold the breath for one second and then blow it out through your mouth. Again, breathe in and hold ... and out again. And again. Continue to breathe like this, nice and slowly, in and out, until you achieve a steady rhythm.

4 Imagine a white healing light entering through the top of your head. As this light flows down through your body, start to feel it relaxing you.

5 Feel the light flow down your neck ... and relax ... then your shoulders ... and relax ... then your arms ... and your hands. All the while you are feeling more and more relaxed.

6 Feel the white healing light flowing down through your chest now ... and relax ... then your stomach and back ... more and more relaxed.

7 Feel relaxed now as the light reaches down through your hips, your thighs, your knees, your calves and down into your feet. Feel this warm, white, healing and relaxing light flowing into every single part of your body.

8 Feel it wash over you ... inside ... and now outside ... flowing over every part of your body, washing away any negativity, taking away any aches and pains and replacing it with a feeling of floating and lightness. Feel relaxed everywhere ... relax ... relax.

9 Now you find yourself floating in a bubble of air, soft and gentle around you. You feel safe and completely secure inside this bubble. Gradually you begin to be aware of a loving presence floating towards you.

10 As this presence gets closer to you, you know instinctively that this loving presence is your guardian angel.

11 This loving energy is so familiar to you. You recall a memory and remember the feeling of being held gently in the arms of your loving guardian angel – your guardian and protector.

12 Take a moment to enjoy the feeling of your guardian angel's total, unconditional love for you and you alone.

13 Merge with this love, luxuriate in the loving arms of your angel, feel this love flood through your very being, just as you imagined the white healing light. Stay like this a while and savour the experience. Enjoy this feeling for as long as you want. When you're ready, continue.

14 Take a good look at the angel in front of you. Your angel smiles at you and you feel perfectly at ease and full of peace. Does your angel show themselves to you as male or female? Look closely now, and wait until you have the answer you seek.

15 Now ask your angel their name. The name could be anything at all, so don't be surprised at the answer. Is the name familiar to you? Is it a name that is new to you?
Take this name now.

16 Spend a few moments with your angel, and ask that they give you a message to help you with your life right now. Take as long as you need.

17 When you're ready, look up and smile at your angel and feel the angelic energy start to pull away.

18 Your angel has their arms held out in a gesture that reassures you that you can call on this angelic energy any time you wish. You are happy, reassured and confident. You are ready to face whatever life brings you.

19 In your own time, come back into the room. Open your physical eyes. You are now wide awake ... wide awake.

20 Spend a few moments going over your experience in your mind. What was your angel's name? Were they male or female? What was your special message and what did it mean to you at this moment in your life?

21 As soon as you're ready, make notes about your experience. Write down the angel's name and any messages that they gave you.

22 Draw any images that came mind during the experience, or that occur to you now. Be sure not to forget to date your notes so that you can refer back to them.

HOW DO PEOPLE SEE ANGELS?

Many people see angels as human-type figures with wings, and others see twinkling lights or bands of rainbow-coloured lights.

I've had people tell me about angels they have seen that are the size of 'fairies', and others have seen angels as large as 'giants'. People see these magnificent beings with their heads through the roof of the house and their feet through the floor. Traditional reports of angels include beings of fire, and grotesque figures with hundreds of pairs of eyes.

Angels don't mind how we 'imagine' them. They are comfortable and happy with our images and understand them to be representations of themselves. Angels have no egos and have no wish to be worshipped as gods. As humans I think it is important for us to have some images in our mind –

our own personal representation of the angels and how they look to us. If you think about it right now, what is an angel to you?

EXERCISE: See your angel meditation

Read through the meditation a few times to familiarize yourself with it, then go ahead. Don't worry if you don't get it exactly.

1 Sit in a quiet room and close your eyes. Take three deep, cleansing breaths by breathing in through your nose and blowing the breath out through your mouth. Then breathe nice and normally. Feel yourself becoming more relaxed.

2 Imagine you are in a beautiful garden. This garden is a safe and happy place, full of deep peace and love. You comfortable here.

3 Spend a few moments creating the perfect garden around you. What can you see? Are there flowers? Can you see trees in your vision? Water? Birds?

4 Find a place to sit in your garden and wait for the angel to approach you. Up ahead of you the image of an angel is beginning to form. Look carefully at it. Is the angel emerging from a light or a doorway of some sort? Do they appear in colour? Do they have wings? Do they appear with clothing? Can you see their feet? Look around and see if there are colours or shapes around the angel. Are they carrying anything? Is any other symbolism attached to the figure that you see before you?

5 Then the angel sends love towards you. Feel this unconditional love. Spend a few moments enjoying this wonderful energy. When you're ready, the angel will begin to pull back again. Then, in your own time, open your eyes and bring yourself gently back into the room. Recall where you are in the here and now and 'be' sitting back in your chair.

6 Make as many notes as you can remember. What did the angel look like? What did the angel feel like? Remember, the purpose of the exercise is to 'see' an angel.

7 Next take a pencil and make some sketches of what you can remember. Don't worry about your drawing skills, just draw. If you have coloured pencils, use these to make any impressions you might have. When you have finished, date your work and save it.

WHAT IS THE ROLE OF AN ANGEL?

An angel's role in our human existence is fairly straightforward. They protect and they love, but this takes on many forms. Generally, angels help us when we are trying to solve our own problems, without taking over. Remember that our life problems help us to grow. Anything that gives angels power over humans is not allowed, and anything that means they are trying to make someone do something they don't want to do is also not permitted.

ANGEL SECRET

Angels love to help us to achieve our goals but prefer to act as co-creators rather than magicians. Ask your angels to bring into your life people who can help you with your problems rather than to solve your problems for you. Imagine how empowered you will feel when you achieve your own goals ... with a little help from your friends.

WHAT CAN ANGELS DO?

What they can do	What they can't do
Send us feelings of love and support	Bring us the winning lotto numbers
Perform dramatic rescues when 'it's not our time'	Solve all our problems
Appear to warn us of danger and steer us away from hazards	Make someone fall in love with us
Provide important information to help us with decision-making	Achieve our goals for us
Bring human support and guidance when we need it most	Interfere with our life lessons
Help us to help ourselves	Spy on our neighbours
Mend things	Hurt and harm others
Assist with healing	Manipulate the free will of ourselves and others
Be our friends	Force us to work in their interest
Substance	Function
Matter	Energy

GIVING THE ANGELS PERMISSION TO HELP

Consider the point about manipulating free will. What does this mean? Imagine you create your first garden and you are very proud of your efforts. If your new neighbour, who incidentally is a great gardener, came round to your house and started moving plants about without permission, you would quite rightly get cross. Why are they messing about with your things?

Let's now look at the situation a little differently. With your new garden you have found a few difficulties, so you pop around to your neighbour and ask their advice. Your neighbour might make a few suggestions and then you can decide if you wish to follow their advice or not. It would be your choice, your own free will.

So, if we use the same rule with angels, we can see that we have to invite the angels to work with us. As humans we have the divine right to free will and freedom of choice, and as long as you don't try to manipulate the free will of others (or break any laws) then most things are OK.

How do I give this permission?

Simply ask out loud for help or support with individual things, or ask for help at the beginning of each day. You could write down your request, call on God directly in the form of a prayer, or perform some sort of ritual. You could also indicate your permission by wearing an angel pin, carrying an angel coin or a worry stone (a pebble or crystal into which you project your worries), or placing angel figurines in your home, car and place of work.

TRUE LIFE STORY:
SAVED FROM A CAR

One day I decided to visit my mother. It was a lovely day and because her home was close by I thought I would walk. I decided to listen to some music as I walked and plugged in my earphones.

I came up to a crossing but wasn't really paying attention. A car came speeding towards me but, as it did so, someone yanked me out of the way and right out of the path of the car. I felt the pull with so much force that the lady in the car just looked at me with total shock on her face. How I missed that car I'll never know.

The really strange thing is that I never saw who pulled me out of the path of that car that day because when I turned round there was no one there. I guess it must have been an angel!

EXERCISE: Ask the angels to help you

How would you like to indicate your permission to the angels? Do you want to read or say specific words to your own guardian angels? This is, perhaps, one of the most direct ways of giving permission.

1 Choose your words carefully and write them down. Remember to say thank you after your request. Here are some examples of the sort of thing you might say:

• Angels, I love my collection of white feathers – please bring more as signs that you are close. Thank you in love.

• Angels, I love it when I feel you around me and it makes me flutter with excitement, but I felt frightened when I heard a noise in the kitchen last night, so would prefer that you don't indicate your presence in that way. Thank you in love.

• Angels, I really enjoyed the dream with an angel message last week and am happy with this sort of communication in the future. Thank you in love.

• Angels, I am nervous about feeling a physical touch and would prefer that we explore other ways of communicating with each other. Thank you in love.

2 Do you have other ideas of your own for giving permission? Are there things you want to do, say or even wear?

Make notes of these too and then date your experiences. If you wish, read out your request to the angels now.

As with the other exercises, write up your final requests in a notebook – leaving space to add others at a later date.

ANGEL NOTEBOOK OR JOURNAL

When we write things down we reinforce the message in our minds. Committing something to paper helps us to bring that 'something' into our lives. It becomes more permanent or fixed as part of our intention. Your angel notes are special and need to be cherished in a special place.

Look out for a hard-cover notebook and cover it with sticky-backed plastic decorated in a suitable pattern. Another thing you might try is to stick your notes (taken from your angel exercises or experiences) in a scrapbook. Cover the scrapbook in pretty angel wrapping paper. Alternatively, a loose-leaf binder may be more your thing. Be inspired when creating this most basic of angel tools, your angel notebook – but have fun with it. I want you to love doing this.

Here are some different ways of using your notebook:

• Write down a list of all the things that you would like an angel to help you with in your life. Remember what they can and can't do. List at least 20 things, then date your notes and add them to your notebook. Make sure you leave space to add notes about how they have helped you with your list, and tick things off as they come about.

• Write down any angel experiences or encounters that you have, or that you hear about.

• Write down any inspirational poetry you find or any that you feel inspired to write.

• Write down any inspirational thoughts that you may have while reading this book.

• Record experiences you have while performing the meditations and exercises in this book.

• Add pictures from magazines, stickers and images from birthday and Christmas cards that inspire you, especially pictures of angels.

• Record your dreams and any messages that you feel your angels are bringing to you.

No doubt you will come up with lots of ideas of your own. Take care of your angel notebook and keep it safe.

HOW DO ANGELS CONTACT US?

Our angels are in constant communication with us every single day. Of course, that doesn't mean that we are always aware of that contact. I appreciate that if you don't know what you are looking for then it is difficult to know when these contacts take place.

Sometimes our angels' communication is decided by our own personality traits; for example, if you are a very quiet and shy person, a dramatic contact from the other world would be frightening, and they will take this into consideration.

Sometimes their contact with us is dictated by the situation we find ourselves in. If we are in a mess, is it because we created this mess? If our angels jump in too soon and sort it all out, then what will we have learnt from the situation? Challenges in life help to strengthen the soul, giving us more confidence in our own abilities.

LISTENING ANGEL FRIENDS

Have you ever been in difficulties in your life? Of course you have. We all have problems in our lives – it's part of being human. It's great, though, when you have a good friend. Friends give us that shoulder to cry on when times are hard. We all have a person in our lives who tries to tell us how we might handle a situation better or how we should have done something differently. This can be very frustrating. When we're down, we don't always want that 'smarty-pants know-all' to tell us what we did wrong. The best friends are ones that listen – just listen. Angels are the friends who listen the best.

TRUE LIFE STORY:
TOUCHED BY AN ANGEL

When I was 14, I was lying in bed one day when I suddenly I felt a hand on my shoulder. I immediately turned round only to find my back was against the wall. At the time I was terrified of ghosts, and as a very young child I had always slept with a light on, yet I never felt any fear from this experience. I always felt it must have been my angel.

ANGEL FEATHERS

Little white feathers have become the angel's prettiest sign. Feathers appear when we need them the most, but they don't have to be white. I am sure that those industrious angels will use whatever is easily to hand and that might mean a bright pink feather or even a black feather. Black feathers do not mean something bad will happen. Ask for a feather sign. The feather might turn up when you least expect it.

How can you tell if a feather is an angel feather or not? An angel feather is always one that appears just when you need it the most, or it may appear after you have asked for a sign.

Collect your angel feathers and save them as if they were precious jewels. You can gather them in a pretty jar or box or use them to decorate things. I often give my feathers away to those who want a sign. I pop them into an envelope with a letter or greetings card and you can do the same. How else might you use your angel feathers? Make a list in your notebook for fun.

COINCIDENCES AND MANIFESTATION

Asking for a sign can mean many things. Have you ever thought of a person and had that same person ring you later in the day? Angel coincidences or synchronicity ('meaningful coincidences'), happen all the time. Perhaps the most appropriate sign from your own angels is for you to have synchronicity in your own life.

Let's look at the word 'ask' once again. Asking for what you want is important for it to manifest in your life, so ask your angels for what you want. Always ask for 'the most suitable solution' after your request, then allow for the angels to come up with an even better plan than the one you considered yourself.

Sometimes you can bring coincidences into your life by creating the vision first of all. Decide what you want, write it down, create an angel manifestation poster (see the exercise on page 33) and then ask your angels to help you bring about your chosen goals.

ANGELS IN YOUR GARDEN

People often have angel experiences in outdoor spaces. There's something about that relaxing atmosphere which makes it particularly conducive to having an angel visitation (a real visit from an angel), particularly on a warm summer's day. How can you make the most of your experience, or even encourage one?

Even if you only have a yard, or room for a chair by your front door, most people have a tiny outdoor space they can decorate. It's fun and easy to create your own angel meditation area by collecting together a few natural items and many objects you already own.

CREATE AN ANGEL GARDEN SANCTUARY

First you need a chair, a bench or perhaps an old log. A natural basket chair is wonderful. Back it into a corner or against a wall. If you feel inspired, you could even paint an old junk-shop chair and create some beautiful flowered cushions to bring outside when the weather is dry. If you're lucky enough to have a 'hidden' corner in your garden, this is the perfect place to create a meditation 'room'. Maybe you could turn your chosen spot into a secret place by shielding it. Line up rows of

scented plants in pots, or screen it off with an old gate, a rose arch and a hand-painted sign. Even the smallest piece of trellis will create the feeling of a private space, or you could use netting or knotted rope.

Naturally, you will want to add some pretty lights for warmer evenings. Candlelight is lovely. Scented tea-lights and candles in glasses are especially suitable in the garden. Look for pretty holders, or paint old jam jars with glass paints. Christmas lights in plain white or gentle natural colours look magical when strung from trees or over an arch, fence or gateway; experiment to get the mood just right. Coloured bulbs are especially mood-enhancing when sited under shrubs.

Sound is very important in your sacred space and water is very easy to add to your garden. Creating the right atmosphere is essential and nothing sets the mood like the sound of trickling water. If space is tight, fill a pretty old dish with pebbles and crystals and place it by your front door or even on a windowsill. Keep it topped up with fresh water so it glistens in the sun (rinse it out every now and again to keep it fresh).

Add some garden angel statues or fairy figurines. Let your imagination go wild. Your space is magical because you create the atmosphere with little bits and bobs. Add a wind chime or two. Gift shops and garden centres sell natural bamboo chimes, or create your own using shells strung together on string. You can drill holes in shells using a hand drill, or choose shells with natural holes. Also look out for pebbles with natural holes in them (traditionally these are doorways to other realms).

ANGEL CLOUDS

Watching the clouds pass by is another great way to spot angels. A comfortable spot is very important even if you are just lying on an old blanket. Cirrus (long fingers of cloud above 18,000 feet) or altostratus (long formations of cloud between 6,000 and 20,000 feet) are particularly beautiful and angel-like. It is easier to lie down on the ground, but it also works if you are lying on a recliner. Relax your eyes and gaze softly at the sky, being careful not to stare at the sun. Watch as the clouds blend softly together. Can you spot an angel wing, or an angel's head surrounded by a glowing halo? Watching clouds helps to put you in a daydreaming state of mind. You might even receive inspiration from your angel while you do this.

TRUE LIFE STORY:
ANGEL VOICES

A few years ago I decided to sit outside in a quiet corner of my garden. It was late and the weather wasn't as good as I'd hoped, but I carried on regardless. It was really gusting and showery but I snuggled under a quilt with a cup of tea. Despite the weather I was quite cosy.

I was hoping to feel inspiration from my angels so had a notepad and pen ready just in case. Just before midnight the wind dropped completely and the atmosphere became calm and peaceful. It was then that I heard singing. It was breathtakingly beautiful and the voice seemed to come from everywhere and nowhere – and then it stopped, almost as soon as it had begun. The voice really touched my heart and I knew it was a gift. At that moment I knew for sure that I'd had my first angel encounter.

DAYDREAMING

We can naturally fall into the state of consciousness called 'daydreaming' several times a day. This relaxed state of mind is where we manifest, create and imagine, and it's a way of processing the large chunks of information that we receive on a daily basis. This peaceful state of mind also puts us in the perfect condition to receive guidance from our guardian angels.

SIGNS OF ANGELS' PRESENCE

Angels show they are in our lives in many different ways. They love to bring us little visual signs, like the feathers I told you about earlier. They bring messages from our friends and relations (on both sides of life) and they also bring scents and sounds. Angel music (the sound of the heavenly choir) is rare, but can sometimes be heard when reassurance is needed the most, during the loss of a loved one.

ANGEL SECRET

Sometimes angels work with humans to help bring messages of comfort to others. Be an angel messenger today. Share a smile or a few kind words with everyone you meet.

TRUE LIFE STORY: A FINAL SALUTE

Mum passed away two weeks after her 77th birthday in a local hospice. My four sisters and I were all with her in her final moments. Following her passing, my sisters and I left the room and the nurses explained we could say a last goodbye to Mum if we wanted to. My eldest sister has hearing difficulties but as we left the room she commented on how lovely and appropriate the angelic music was that she'd heard playing in the room. My sisters and I all looked at each other, stunned. There had been no music playing in the room – at least none of us had heard it. She explained that the music was unlike anything she had ever heard before (or since).

EXERCISE: Make an angel manifestation poster

If you could have anything in your life what would it be? Your goals only need to be realistic 'to you'. You have to believe in them. Try not to add limitations on your goals or worry about how they might happen. Hand over the solution to your angels and follow their lead and suggestions.

1 Write down the numbers 1 to 20 on a large sheet of paper. List 20 things that you would like to achieve in the next 12 months. These goals can be anything you want.

2 Read down the list and pick the top five. Highlight them in a bold marker pen. Read them again. Which ones make you feel really excited?

3 Pick, say, two to start with. Get yourself two large pieces of white paper. At the top of the page, write down your goals in large letters with a felt marker pen. Each page has its own goal.

4 Then write underneath, 'I am really happy, angels, that I have achieved my goal of ...', and write in a little more detail about your goal, as if you have already achieved it.

5 Decorate your paper. Place a smiling photo of yourself in the middle, and add photos of family and friends around you, particularly those you want involved in the plan or goal.

6 Find photos to represent your goal – a plane, car, uniform for a new job, exotic location, for example – then place them around the outside.

7 When you have finished, put your 'angel manifestation poster' in a prominent place, where you will see it every day.

8 Sit down right now and absorb yourself into your image. Ask your guardian angel to help you. 'See' very strongly that you are in this situation of your choosing. 'Feel' the emotions you would feel if you were actually there or had achieved your goals. At all times know your angel is by your side helping to create exciting opportunities to further your goal – stay alert and follow through any likely situation that arises.

THE SPHERES OF ANGELS

Over the years, many ancient scholars have tried to classify the angels and sort them into different groups. These groups have been called the 'angelic hierarchy' or the 'spheres of angels'. The angels who work with humankind as the guardian angels are the ones closest to us, and the angels at the top of the tree are the angels who work right next to God.

The name 'angel' is thought to come from the Greek word *angelos* which means 'messenger'. In the Bible, the angel Gabriel visited Mary with a message – he informed her that she was pregnant with the baby Jesus. This important task makes Gabriel one of two of the best known of all the angels (the other is Archangel Michael, the warrior angel – a protector associated with churches and other places of worship).

THE ARCHANGELS

The archangels are the best known of all the angels, although their names and the spellings do change slightly in different parts of the world. For more information on Metatron see pages 70–71, and for Raphael see page 112–113.

Here are ten of the best known and their traditional roles:

THE THREE SPHERES OF THE ANGELS

First sphere (working closest to God)	Second sphere (looking after the planets)	Third sphere (working closest to humankind)
1 Seraphim	4 Dominions	7 Principalities
2 Cherubim	5 Virtues	8 Archangels
3 Thrones	6 Powers	9 Guardian angels

- **Ariel** In charge of animals and birds. Archangel Ariel is also in charge of the nature kingdom, which includes the fairies (also called the angels of the earth).

- **Gabriel** The messenger angel, Archangel Gabriel is in charge of communication and the patron of postal workers.

- **Haniel** Archangel Haniel helps with all your magical learning, and works with crystals, herbs and the power of the moon.

- **Jeremiel** A kind and loving angel who sends you messages in dreams, Archangel Jeremiel helps you to connect to your past lives.

- **Metatron** Archangel Metatron was once a human man called Enoch. He is the angel who records all human thoughts and deeds and this information is stored in the heavenly 'Book of Life'.

- **Michael** Often seen in paintings and statues in churches, Archangel Michael is the head of the heavenly armies, so is strong and powerful and usually seen carrying his sword of protection.

- **Raphael** The angelic healer, Archangel Raphael works with doctors, nurses and healers of all kinds. He is also the patron of travellers.

- **Sandalphon** Because of the good work the human prophet Elijah performed on earth, God made him into the Archangel Sandalphon. Carries human prayers up to God.

- **Uriel** The healer of the Earth Archangel Uriel helps to bring order after earthquakes, floods and fire.

- **Zadkiel** The creative force behind many great works, Archangel Zadkiel helps with ideas and inspiration in your own endeavours.

'All angels work with me now'

WORKING WITH ANGELS

'He will give his angels charge of you to guard you in all your ways'

Psalms 91: 11–12

The simplest way to connect with your angels is just to ask them something, and I remind you of this over and over again in this book. However, most of us find it easier and a whole lot more fun to connect to the angels using a few 'tools of the trade'. I like to connect with angels in a mixture of ways, and the following are my favourites. I'll discuss them in detail on the pages that follow:

- **Angel meditation:** Allowing yourself to achieve a deeply relaxed state of mind.

- **Affirmations:** Using an affirmation can help to create encouraging and optimistic thoughts about your goals.

- **Rituals:** Following an action (such as lighting a candle) while saying your affirmation will certainly help to make it more memorable.

- **Altars and displays:** Arranging your personal effects in such a way that they are a constant reminder of your links with your angels.

- **Candles:** Lighting a candle is a ritualistic way of 'opening to the light' (light/love = the highest vibration). Therefore candles are useful for meditations and your angel ceremonies.

- **Oils and incense:** I love to work with pure aromatherapy oils and there are many that are suitable for your angel work.

- **Crystals:** These beautiful, natural objects are a joy to behold, and are sources of untold power.

- **Feathers:** These are probably one of the most important of all the 'tools'; they are the chosen sign from the angels themselves.

ANGEL MEDITATION

By putting yourself into a deeply relaxed state of mind you can reach out further to your angels and they can pull a little closer to you. Your angels might also appear in your dreams, as mine do.

Although our angels are in constant contact with us, our busy lives and cluttered minds often miss their messages and signs. Angels exist in a different dimension to humankind. They are like 'thought' to us, and rarely visible to the human eye. For us to see them, either we have to change our own level of consciousness or the angels have to do the same. That's where meditation comes in. Meditation puts us into a 'different' level of consciousness, making it easier for the angels to reach out to us.

PREPARATION

To meditate, you need to clear your mind of as much thought-clutter as possible – stem the flow of random thoughts. I like to relax for a few minutes and write down all the 'jobs' that my mind throws out at me. Some of the things that we carry around in our mind with us all the time, and are probably not aware of, might include shopping lists, timetables,

things we have to do every day (like take certain pills, for example), collecting people and dropping them off, remembering people's birthdays or what time your favourite TV programme starts, and so on. If you write these things down, your mind will no longer need to 'hold them' and you will find it easier to relax.

Meditating means you are putting your body (and, with luck, your mind) into a state of deep relaxation. The more you practise the more relaxed you become and the deeper the meditation will be. Deeper meditative states produce more paranormal types of phenomena; so the more you practise this the better you will get, and the more and the greater will be the spiritual rewards.

RELAXATION TECHNIQUES

Classic relaxation techniques might include seeing yourself going down a staircase, floating higher and higher, or moving down in a lift. These are all 'tricks' to help the mind to relax into deeper and deeper levels. Another way to relax the body is to imagine your mind relaxing each body part one at a time (either starting at the head and working down, or starting at the toes and working up), stopping as your mind reaches each part of your body and you instruct it (in your thoughts) to relax. For example, 'Relax your toes ... wiggle them a little, then relax, relax. Next your foot ... relax your foot ... watch your foot becoming more and more relaxed.

All the meditations in this book give you suggestions for ways of setting up your meditation ritual. You might wish to have a special chair in your house where you always meditate; perhaps you will decide always to light a candle before you start or to put your chair in a certain position.

Other rituals might include playing music before or during your meditation session, or having a cosy blanket nearby to make sure you keep warm. Another good idea is to make a recording of the words of the meditation so that you can play it as you meditate. This way you'll be able to set a relaxed pace to the meditation. If you are new to the meditation, this will also ensure that you don't miss any of the steps.

All these things will help to ensure a successful outcome. Your mind and body will become familiar with the routine and relax into the exercise more easily in time as familiarity takes over.

RECORD YOUR SESSIONS

Always make a note of your sessions. Keep a record of any experiences you have or things you see during your angel meditations and remember to date your entries. Leave a few lines or half a page blank under your entries in case you need to add extra notes at a later date.

ALTARS AND DISPLAYS

Arranging your personal angel-inspired objects in beautiful ways helps to remind you of the connection you have with your angels. The objects are not angels themselves but help to arouse angelic thoughts. Many people believe that their angel altars become infused with angel energy, and I'm sure they are right.

Lots of people like to use the word 'altar' to describe their angel-inspired displays, but if that sounds too religious to you then it's fine to call it an 'arrangement' or whatever you like. An 'angel altar' is a collection of angel-themed objects, lovingly gathered and displayed together, to create an 'intent' to do or be something. People use them for healing purposes, as places for prayer and meditation, or to create changes in their lives.

Like the rituals and meditations, your display will focus your 'will' and therefore your energy, thereby sending that power towards your chosen goal. Every time you clean your display or admire it, you increase the energy towards your original intent. Creation and manifestation goals are particularly enhanced by a sacred arrangement of specially chosen objects; that's why it's important to keep your display fresh, with flowers changed and crystals washed and shiny. Dust says 'I no longer care about this arrangement, so therefore I am no longer focused on my goal or the reason I created my display in the first place'. Keep it looking nice and, once its purpose is complete, create something new.

Make sure your displays always look exciting and interesting to you. If you get bored with looking at your arrangement, it's time to add some new objects or just change everything around.

ANGEL ALTARS

Any 'angel altar'– that is, one in which you are requesting the angels to help with a particular problem – would usually need an angel of some sort added to the display. You can use anything at all with an angel image on it – a book, cards, figurine or coins, or something you have made yourself.

AFFIRMATIONS AND RITUALS

An affirmation is a positive declaration. It can be something you say or something you read. You can create a poster with words on it or a card that you carry around, or just add the words to your computer screensaver.

AFFIRMATIONS

Affirmations are best when they are phrased as if you were already doing what you want to do (rather than imagining it happening in the future). So phrases start 'I am doing' rather than 'I would like to' (you will soon get used to this).

RITUALS

Rituals can help affirm your goals and wishes and also be used to create closure on a situation. In most cases, it's OK for you to create your own words and phrases. I have made suggestions in every instance, but go ahead and change things if you want (or your angels inspire you) to do so. Try to remember to address your message to 'someone' (God, your guardian angel, the goddess, the supreme creator – whichever feels right to you). Make sure you state your purpose clearly, and then end with a thank you (to ritualistically close down your 'session').

Rituals can be spell-like, in that they are performed to help bring about a positive outcome or change in a situation. Of course you can just ask the angels to help you if you want to, with no rituals at all. But creating an affirmation where you light and then blow out a candle, make a pattern with crystals or burn certain types of oil works in the same way that your angel altar does – it helps to fix your message or request firmly in your mind, and draws together all the universal energy you need to manifest your required outcome.

With all ritual work, remember that you can ask for the angels to help bring energy to a situation as long as it doesn't hurt anybody else or interfere with the free will of another person. The real magic involves changing yourself – for the better. Now that is totally under your control. The best rituals are those where we need healing energy, inspiration or help in bringing about a positive change in our own lives (a new job, for example).

CANDLES

Light a candle at the beginning of any ritual, and blow it out at the end (to ritualistically close down your meditation/ritual/spell after working with your angel altars/displays). You can do this every time if you wish. Use candles in glasses or 'safety candles' (tea-lights) to make sure there aren't any accidents.

I often suggest that you light a candle before meditating. You can also use candles on your displays and altars. Below are a few suggested colours and their meanings. If your angel inspires you to use a different colour, then work with that – trust your angel instincts.

Take care not to close your eyes during rituals/meditations if there are pets or young children around, or a breeze through an open window. Even better, make sure your family are looked after so that you can relax in peace. Safety comes first – then you can enjoy your experiences.

CANDLE COLOURS AND THEIR USES

Colour	Angel	Meaning or use
Black	Archangel Michael	Use to take something away
Pink	Archangel Jophiel	Unconditional love
Blue	Archangel Raphael	Healing
Green	Archangel Ariel	Money/animals
Red	Archangel Azrael	Passion/romance
Yellow	Archangel Chamuel	Happiness/children
White	All the angels	Use in place of any other candle

OILS AND INCENSE

Angels respond very well to the perfume and vibrational energy of natural oils (made from plants, flowers or fruits). Some are suitable for use in an oil burner (the scent fills the room as a few drops in water are gently warmed); others are suitable for use directly on the body (massaged in using a 'carrier oil'). You can also burn incense sticks.

ANGELIC PERFUME

Angels respond very well to aromatherapy oils. When angels make an appearance, they often arrive on a cloud of perfume. Most common is the very strong smell of flowers such as roses, lilies or hyacinths. The scent of flowers is a spiritual gift for you and a way of them letting you know they are around you. Another favourite is vanilla, a comforting smell for many people – the scent of baby powder, ice cream and custard.

When performing any angelic rituals or meditation, or simply creating a sanctuary space in your home, you can infuse the space with the scent and energy of frankincense. Frankincense oil creates a high energy room and I have found that it raises the vibration of the space, making it easier for your angels to reach 'down' to you. You can add a few drops of pure frankincense aromatherapy oil into water in the top of an oil burner, available from health shops and gift stores (follow the manufacturer's instructions).

You might also find pure frankincense incense sticks, which also work well. The only other incense I use for angel work is the natural 'marsarla' incense Nag Champa (I love the Sai Baba Nag Champa incense, which is hand-rolled with a sandalwood base and blended natural resins, gums, flowers and oils – beautiful and pure). Create your atmosphere!

A WORD OF CAUTION

Make sure you check out a professional website or book on aromatherapy oils to ensure that any oils you use are safe for you and your family to infuse into the atmosphere. Some oils can be poisonous or dangerous, so always check the label before using.

CRYSTALS FOR ANGEL RITUALS

I love to buy crystals and – even better – to receive them as gifts (as many of mine have been). I have them on my desk, windowsills and tables. I love to mix up the tumbled (smooth-edged) stones in big angel-decorated bowls (some of mine have angels sitting on the edge of a dish). A cut-glass bowl filled with mixed crystals looks especially beautiful.

I also have larger pieces as part of my altars and displays, which are all over the house. Feathers –Angels leave feathers as gifts for many reasons. You can carry them around, store them in a pretty box or jar, or give them away.

CRYSTAL POWER

These 'powerhouses' make you feel excited just by looking at them. Who knows the force contained within the crystal? We are only just scratching the surface of their uses. There are many books that outline the attributes of the different crystals. What I've discovered is that, as human beings, we too vibrate at different rates depending on our moods, health and spiritual growth, so different crystals will appeal to us on different days. By all means work with a crystal book to select your stones if you want to, but how much better would it be to ask your angels to guide you?

When choosing crystals, always use your own instinct; don't be restricted in your choice by an over-eager shop assistant, or a well-meaning 'crystal-expert' friend. Many people feel that the crystal chooses its owner. The crystal seems to call out to you. Likewise, over time I have passed on (or sold) some of my own precious collection when I have no longer felt drawn to them (or perhaps they are no longer drawn to me).

Like people, crystals come and go in our lives. They like to stay a while, brighten up our lives and sparkle and shine, exciting our senses. Then, like a polite guest, they always know when it's time to leave. Let them go with love and send them on their way to continue doing good in the world, knowing that new and more suitable crystals will fill their place.

CHOOSING YOUR CRYSTALS

If you're lucky enough to have a crystal shop near to where you live, then this is the best way to select your working tools. Many places sell odd crystals these days; even if they don't specialize, you can pick up the small, rounded crystals from many gift shops. Tourist shops (especially those near caves which are open to the public, or those next to ancient buildings or museums) may also hold a selection, so it's worth checking out the gift shop.

First of all, I suggest you walk along a display using only your eyes. Does any particular piece stand out to you? Maybe the colour is particularly appealing or you are attracted to the shape. Ask if you can pick it up. Now hold in your hands and turn it round, examining all angles. How does it catch the light? Do the colours change as you move it around?

Next close your eyes. Take the energy of the crystal into your body, asking the angels to show you how you might use the crystal – healing, protection, inspiration? Watch as images form in your mind; now ask the angels 'Should I take the crystal home?' 'Does it "belong" to me?' Of course, we never completely own a crystal; we merely borrow it for a while, as a gift from the Earth.

Make sure the crystal is within your budget and never be tempted to spend more than you have readily available, although some shop owners are prepared to trade or reduce the price on larger items. The more often you buy from the shop the more likely the owner is to reduce the price of something that appeals to you.

People who work with crystals on a regular basis, those who are drawn to sell crystals, are often intuitive and will know when a crystal 'belongs' to someone – they too may see or feel the connection between the two of you. They may be prepared to put the crystal to one side for you so that you can pay for it over several weeks. All you have to do is ask!

CLEANSING YOUR CRYSTALS

Many people believe that crystals collect energy, both positive and negative, and that it's important to cleanse them from time to time. Cleansing is a way of purifying your stone, or neutralizing it, and there are many different ways of doing this.

Ideally, you should rinse your crystals in a natural stream – a crystal clear mountain stream would be perfect. Failing this, rinsing them in a bowl of spring water works almost as well. Even a running tap is better than nothing; keeping them free of dust is important. Take care, though, as some crystals are particularly fragile and won't be happy sitting around in water, which may break them down. So give them a quick rinse and leave them to dry naturally if you can on a sunny windowsill or outside if it's safe to do so (where they won't be taken by animals, birds or children). My cats love to bat them around the house, so poster putty can be useful in displaying them.

Another way to cleanse (although not clean) your crystals is to pull them through a plume of smoke. Hold them carefully and bring them through the smoke of a candle flame – making sure you don't get burnt – an incense stick or a smudge stick. (A 'smudge' is a bundle of dried herbs, usually white sage, sometimes mixed with other herbs like lavender or sweetgrass. The smudge stick, sometimes called a wand, is often used to purify and cleanse a room, item or person.)

CHARGING CRYSTALS

Once your crystals are clear, you need to recharge them. Sunlight on its own is good, and you can also leave them out in a full moon to draw in the moon's energy overnight. You can also charge them using your 'intent' or 'will'. Hold the crystal in your hand and imagine all the power of the universal energy flowing into your body through your head and out through your hands into the crystal.

Say: *Crystal I charge thee with universal energy and with the power of my guardian angel (three times). With love and thanks*

DEDICATING YOUR CRYSTALS

Many people like to give individual crystals a specific task – the 'car protector crystal', the 'take care of my cat crystal' or the 'look after my desk at work crystal'.

To dedicate your crystal, first hold it in the palm of your hand, then place your other hand over the top of the crystal. In your mind, imagine clearly your crystal in its new place or home performing its new task. Talk to the crystal, explaining exactly what you want it to do and why. Send this image to the crystal using telepathy

(mind-to-mind conversation) so
that your crystal is clear on what is
expected of it.

Next bring the crystal up to your
heart and hold it next to the skin so
that it feels the beat of your heart.
Hold it here for a full minute, then
bring it down again and draw it
through the smoke of an incense
stick or candle.

Say: *I dedicate this crystal to ... (add
details here) with all my love and
with the power of my guardian angel
(three times). With love and thanks*

COMMON CRYSTALS AND THEIR USES

Crystal	Typical use
Clear quartz	A powerful charger crystal (use with all rituals), helping to boost all other crystals it works with (use alongside other crystals or alone)
Angelite	Useful in all angel rituals (particularly magical)
Rose quartz	Love
Tiger's eye	Rituals for teenagers
Obsidian	A grounding stone, helping to bring you 'down to earth'
Amethyst	Protection and psychic work
Jasper	Freedom (to remove yourself from an unwanted situation)
Citrine	Problem solving, mind puzzles
Moonstone	A traditional stone for balancing women's bodies/pregnancy/hormones

FEATHERS

Feathers are probably the most important sign your angels will bring you. White feathers are the angels' regular 'hello' sign to let you know that they are around. Your white feather might be large and straight like a quill, or medium-sized and curled like a swan feather, or maybe tiny and fluffy like that from a baby bird – all these 'count' as a sign.

Feathers usually mean:

- I am here, I am with you
- I have not forgotten you
- You are not alone
- I am protecting you
- Yes, that sign, that touch, that feeling ... it was me
- I love you
- I am by your side in your hour of need
- I hear you
- I watch over you
- I was here
- We are working on the problem
- We are aware of the situation
- Your angels are bringing you the energy to cope with the situation
- Angels are real
- I have your loved one safe
- Your deceased loved one is here

When you see a feather in answer to a question, remember to say 'thank you' and pick up the feather to take home with you if you want to.

ANGEL WINGS

When people see angels with wings, it is usually more for our benefit. The angels make themselves appear in a way that will bring us comfort. Angels are actually beings of light rather than souls like humans. They have no need of wings to fly.

TRUE LIFE STORY:
FEATHER IN THE SHOP

The last couple of nights I've been asking my angels for guidance. I walked into a shop to do some crystal hunting and spotted a 'pudding stone', and lying in the bowl was a blue feather. I asked the owner if she had placed the feather there and she said no. I took this as a sign and I bought the stone. I took the feather home, too!

WHAT TO DO WITH YOUR FEATHERS

If you're creative, you can use your angel feathers in all sorts of fun ways. You can use a large feather as a bookmark, stick feathers to the edge of a lampshade or glue them around your photo frames (especially if you want the angels to protect someone). Some people keep a special box or jar especially for their angel feathers, but I like to pass them on to others who need them. You decide!

WHERE TO FIND ANGEL FEATHERS

You never need to look for angel feathers because they will always find you. Angel feathers turn up in the most unexpected of places and nearly always when you need a sign the most. No doubt you will find special feathers if you walk in your local woods or along the hedgerows, but never fear – if you need a sign it will find you wherever you are.

ASKING FOR A FEATHER

If you really want the angels to bring you a feather you can ask for one. Use the following words to help you: *Angel light, clear bright, bring me an angel feather tonight*

Say the words last thing before you go to sleep. You never know!

TRUE LIFE STORY:
FEATHERS UNDER THE ANGEL FIGURINE

My friends and I became interested in stories of angels a few years ago. One of our group visited Malta and brought back three beautiful gold-and-white angel figurines that had been blessed. I placed mine on my bedside cabinet. I started to say my prayers directly to the angel and I always had the feeling that she was at my side.

I have recently been ill and was bedridden for several weeks and ended up being admitted to hospital for treatment. When I got home I went straight upstairs to my bedroom and there was my angel exactly where I had left her. the room was dusty and the first thing I did was to dust. When I picked up my angel there underneath was a pure white feather. I don't have a duckdown duvet or pillows and no one had been in the room since I went into hospital. It was a mystery.

I was overcome with an overwhelming feeling of happiness and I know that, no matter what happens, my angel will always be there for me.

FEATHER COLOURS AND THEIR MEANINGS

Colour	Meaning
White	The most common of angel gifts. 'I am around you, everything will be OK.'
Black	Most often found during times of crisis. 'I am aware of your current life difficulties and am helping and supporting you.'
Yellow	'Congratulations! Things are going well right now.'
Pink	'Surprise!' Your angels are joining in with the fun in your life or maybe having a little joke – they will laugh with you but never at you.
Blue	'Time for calm and peace in your life.' Find space in your life for serenity by taking a walk by water or meditating.
Red	Passion and love. 'We are helping with matters of the heart.'
Green	'Your angels send you healing.' Help by taking good care of your spiritual and bodily well-being.
Grey	'Although things seem quiet right now, we are working on the problem. Be ready for our signs soon.' Follow your angels' guidance and be patient while they put things into place for you.

'I will look for the angels in my life as I know they are with me even now'

ANGELS AND LOVE

'Everything in my heart I give to you, totally, unconditionally'

Love is the greatest of all our God-given gifts. Without love we feel bereft, lonely, sad. Our angels know everything there is to know about us: the good, the bad, our greatest achievements and our biggest mistakes. Yet an angel's role is never to judge or criticize. Your angels see right into your heart. Knowing your total history in this life and others, your guardian angel brings you total and unconditional love.

Part of the angels' role is to help remove the negative feelings and depressing energies from our lives; they help lighten our moods and lift heavy loads from our shoulders. Love is very important in our lives. When we have love, our bodies glimmer with light and health. We move more quickly, walk a little faster and shine a little more brightly. Our inner glow becomes manifest – everyone can see we are 'in love' with life.

One of the angels' roles on earth is to help bring about this state of mind at all times. The feeling we have for one another is nothing compared to the love we feel for our supreme creator. The angels' function is to help to remind us of the love we hold deep inside ourselves and to help release it as a permanent state of being – to bring in the light, enlightenment or the total state of bliss.

As human souls, we experience many different types of love: love for our partners; the special love we have for our children; and the love we have for our friends. Yet love can often be conditional or dependent on others, and this is why we feel loss without others to love us back.

Love is very much a state of being, but what many people don't understand is that we choose our feelings. We can decide whether to feel happy or sad, excited or worried, confused, understanding, and so on. Instead of blaming others for how you 'feel', remember that their actions only affect you if you let them.

EXERCISE: Create your protective bubble meditation

This exercise will help you feel unconditional love. Put on some loose clothing and stand in a safe place. This might be your living room or your garden – anywhere you can stretch out a bit.

1 Close your eyes and stand with your legs apart. Now reach out your arms and move them around your body in big circles. Take up a big space around you and stretch out your fingers. Bend and sway at the waist.

2 Now stand with your hands down by your sides and your legs closer together. With your eyes still closed, imagine a big white bubble of energy surrounding your body, filling up the space you have just taken up with your arms. The bubble is strong and flexible; see the bubble of energy gently surrounding your entire frame. This bubble is your aura or energy field.

3 Once you can see the bubble in your mind's eye, try to 'puff out' the shape so that it forms a bigger and thicker blanket around you; imagine it and know it is done.

Spend a few minutes doing this so that you are happy with your new, bigger aura bubble. Make it as big as you like.

4 Next, imagine pink, loving energy flowing into the bubble. Ask your guardian angel to help you. The energy is smooth with no ragged edges. This pink flowing energy is pure unconditional love, and it's strong and protective. Take as long as you like doing this.

5 When you're ready, open your eyes and reanimate your body, shaking your arms and legs. Bring your mind back into the room or space.

After the exercise, have a drink to 'ground yourself' back into the here and now. If you ever feel yourself under verbal attack, recreate this exercise in your mind. See again your strong loving bubble of energy that surrounds and protects you. Know that negative energy can't penetrate and only love surrounds you. If you feel strong enough, bounce back loving energy to your 'abuser' – you might be surprised at their reaction!

HOW THE ANGELS LOVE US

Angels show their love for us in many different ways. Sometimes the experiences we feel are subtle and at other times they are very dramatic indeed. Angels can lead us to people we need in our lives and they can also offer protection in the gentlest of ways.

They bring messages in dreams and coincidences, and occasionally with whispered words. Some people feel a hand in their hand or an arm around their shoulder during their time of need. Angels always find a way of reaching out to us.

LOVE YOURSELF

The best way to help the angels bring you love is to begin by loving yourself. All too often that inner babble or noisy chatter is the voice of your own overseeing mind which continues to criticize you constantly in your head. I bet you have heard the sound of your own voice more often than you care to remember. 'You're not good enough.' 'You're too old/young/thin/fat.' 'No one is going to listen to you.' That voice can be frustrating in its persistence.

By changing the negative voice to a positive one you can bring about many changes in your life. Imagine what it must be like to be abused for your whole life by someone who constantly puts you down and doubts your abilities, yet most of us do this to ourselves every single day. We are our own biggest critics. Ask your angel to help stop this self-abuse right now.

POSITIVE THINKING

Our state of mind exists as a result of years of conditioning, mainly through outside influences. Maybe as a child you were told you were the 'clumsy one' or that you would 'never amount to anything'.

Breaking free of these conditioned responses is as simple as changing your habits. Affirmations, those positive phrases said over and over again, will recondition that inner voice. Working with your loving angel is all powerful. Remember, you can achieve your goals with the help of your special friend.

ENCOURAGE YOUR CHAMPIONING ANGEL

The voice is like a little imp sitting on your shoulders. It's the imp that nags away at you all day long. 'You can't do that; you won't cope with that, you're not worthy to do such and such', and so on. Replace the nagging imp with a championing angel; each time you hear a negative comment, counter it with a loving and positive one from your strong and powerful angel. Your angel is so much bigger and stronger and can fight the voice away. Below are a few examples.

Sometimes people use a little humour with this and they imagine the big powerful angel pushing the imp off their shoulders. The imp's protests are persistent, but your sturdy angel can soon control the situation. Only positive and loving comments will get through from now on. You could even imagine the angel putting some sticky tape over the mouth of the imp – whatever helps you to carry out the exercise, especially if it makes you laugh. Have some fun with this and come up with your own images.

BANISH NEGATIVE THOUGHTS

If a negative comment slips into your mind, lift up your shoulders the minute you become aware of what is happening. Stand tall with confidence (even if you feel you are pretending). If necessary, have your angel bring you several positive and loving comments to replace any negative ones. Then practise, practise, practise! Do this for a period of 14 days straight. I'm sure at the end of this time you won't ever want to stop.

INNER VOICES

Old criticizing voice	Change to praising voice
You're useless	You're brilliant
You don't have the experience	You can learn anything you need to know
You'll never be able to manage on your own	You're a strong and capable person
You're too fat to do anything	I eat healthily and care for my body
You're ugly	I'm beautiful/handsome
Nobody likes you	I have many wonderful friends

LOVING THOUGHTS

When you think of your loved ones, always hold the feeling of love in your heart. Always embrace positive thoughts and send positive energy in your mind. Imagine only upbeat and loving thoughts travelling in their direction. People often become what we think of them. See their guardian angel holding them in a tender and devoted hug, even if they are being particularly annoying today!

ANGEL SECRET

It's not easy to like everyone who comes into your life – the angels know this and understand. They do ask you to try to love everyone. It's much harder to love someone you don't like, so you will need to practise. Work as hard as you need to so that you can accept someone for who they are right now.

EXERCISE: Create some loving affirmations

1 Write down or type up some positive sayings. Imagine your guardian angel is like a loving parent or coach supporting your every endeavour. What would that supportive teacher be saying to you right now? Change the saying so that this now comes from you. Make yourself your own loving guide. Begin your affirmations with the word 'I'. Say your affirmations as if they have already happened, rather than something you want to happen in the future. Here are some examples you can use (or create your own):

• I am healthy, happy and full of energy

• I have passed my exams with excellent results

• I have everything I need to achieve my goal

• I have a job that I love

• I am in a loving, secure relationship

2 Cut out your affirmations and place them on the fridge or bedside table. You could even have an affirmation taped to the bathroom mirror – anywhere you will see it every day, or several times a day. Use several at a time, or work on one message that you place everywhere around your home.

TRUE LIFE STORY:
LOVING ANGEL HUG

I'd been separated for a year and then finally my divorce was finalized. After a 12-year marriage I was completely drained both physically and emotionally. My relationship had often been abusive and I was suffering from anxiety and depression.

One night I was sitting up in bed mulling over the following day's plans. I had to go to court to get residency and organize access to my boys. I was not looking forward to facing my ex-husband again. It was then that I considered asking my angels for help. I said to them: 'Right, I haven't asked for help in such a long time, angels, please can you give me some support, keep me strong and help me to relax?'

Straight away I felt a warm energy go right through my body; it started at the top and flowed right down to my feet. It's been so long since I've felt so in tune with my angels that I'd forgotten what an amazing experience it could be. I felt so relaxed that I drifted off into a wonderful deep sleep and woke the following morning feeling calm and relaxed.

Driving to court the next morning, the sun was shining and every song that came on the radio was one that I liked. I was happily singing along to the tunes and it really lifted my spirits. The court experience that day was actually very straightforward and I'm glad to say I won my case. I felt as if a big weight had been lifted off my shoulders and I know that my angels helped me. I know that they were with me and I wouldn't hesitate to ask them for help again in the future.

SOULMATES AND THEIR GIFTS

The archangels are powerful and majestic beings. Their roles are numerous but the archangel who has particular care over loving relationships is Chamuel, who helps to bring soulmates together. There are many different types of soulmate and in each lifetime you spend time with those who can help you learn and grow the most.

Soulmates aren't always romantic partners but may be father and son or even brother and sister. We may have chosen to incarnate with others of our soul group who are best placed to help us learn and grow. How do the people in your life help you? Why not ask your angels to help you make a list of each of your soulmates' gifts to you? For example, your aunt has been ill for many years. She is needy and takes up a lot of your time. You visit her several times a week and even take her shopping. What might her gifts be to you? Unconditional love, compassion?

Maybe your younger brother is always in your bedroom messing around with your things. He and his friends tease you constantly and you can't easily bring your own friends back to the house because he is so embarrassing. What are his gifts – adaptability, endurance, tolerance? After you have made your lists, you will be more aware of how people

have chosen to work with you in this lifetime to help bring these gifts to you. We all help each other. Can you see people with more tolerance knowing how they help you?

It's difficult not to judge another human soul but we are each on our own unique journey and the Earth is full of people at different stages of their journey. We wouldn't expect a baby to drive a car because we know it is above and beyond their capability considering their stage of growth. With patience, that baby soul grows up and with love the soul grows (we hope) into a loving, caring human being.

Using this analogy, look at those around you who are struggling with life. They may be young souls (even in an older body). Looks can be deceiving. Sometimes young children can be the wisest souls of all. It's difficult to know and understand what that other person has had to

live through, and the challenges they have had to face along life's journey. The angels bring the message that life has one important goal. Love is the most important thing of all.

LOVE AFTER LIFE

Love never dies when life ends. The love that we have with those on the other side stays with us our whole life long. Memories are always with us (write them down if you are worried about forgetting). The essence of the person we have lost is always around us – when we think of them still we make that special connection. I hear many stories of people trying to connect to their loved ones from both sides of life. The following true-life story is particularly magical. Rainbows are a wonderful sign that is often used as a message of love from the other side of life. Love and be loved, starting with this side of life.

EXERCISE: Appreciate your soulmates

Close your eyes and think about the people who are in your life right now. These people might be work colleagues, neighbours, cousins, or even someone who works in the local shop. Do you see them regularly? Do they affect your life either negatively or positively?

1 Write the name of someone in your life at the top of a piece of paper. Now close your eyes. Imagine their face in front of you. How do you feel about them? What occasions do you recall when you have interacted? Does this person make you feel happy, sad, frustrated? Every person in your life brings you a gift (although it's not always apparent what the gift might be, especially if you squabble or don't like the person). Write down the gifts that this person brings into your life.

2 Repeat this as many times as necessary, using a separate sheet of paper for each person in your life.

3 After writing down all the names and everyone's gifts, ask your angel to send each person unconditional love. Thank your soulmates for their help. (In some cases, it might even be appropriate to thank them in real life and not just in your mind!)

TRUE LIFE STORY:
AT THE RAINBOW'S END

It's 18 months since Mum passed over. It was Mum's last day, although at the time I didn't realize it; I was sitting by her bed holding her hand in the nursing home, and all I could hear was Christmas carols playing in the background. All of a sudden I could only hear the song 'Somewhere over the rainbow'. It may sound silly but at the time I could swear my Mum was singing this song to me. I felt so much peace listening to the words. The song became very important to me ... like it was our song. Strangely, later on my daughter walked into her kitchen and heard her husband singing the same song, as if he were picking it up too.

Now this is when it gets very strange. My son, my niece Claire and I all heard her four-year-old singing 'Somewhere over the rainbow' while he was sitting in bed. Claire didn't realize that he knew the song and asked him where he'd heard it before. He told her his Granddad was singing along with him at the same time – his deceased Granddad! Well, what a comfort, I know with all my heart that my Dad was waiting to take Mum safely over to the other side.

When we went to sort out her funeral arrangements, I asked if they did a white coffin (I don't even know where that idea came from as it was never discussed with my Mum). They told me that they only had one white one but it had a rainbow on it. I was stunned and immediately burst into tears. Needless to say we bought it. I know Mum sends us all rainbows from time to time to let us know she is around us. Rainbows make me so happy!

'I am loved, I am love'

ANGELS AND CAREERS

'I guide and lead you to fulfilling employment, bringing opportunities manifest'

For many people, their career defines who they are. When asked the question 'Who are you?' or invited to 'Tell me about yourself ', many answer first with their job title: 'I'm a nurse', 'I'm a merchant banker', 'I'm a builder', and so on.

A career doesn't have to be a paid one. One of the most important roles, for example, is that of mother or father. Your career then is 'growing' children and turning them into mature, well-equipped adults. Your career might be that you employ your time in ways that don't require monetary payment (crafts, keeping house, charity work, and so on).

Angels watch over all of these roles and stay by our side during every trial and tribulation. There are angels whose role is to help you be in the right place at the right time to fulfil your career destiny. Each angel also has its own job or special interest.

Angels have awareness of our pre-life plan (the life and lessons we choose for ourselves before birth). Our careers, as with other life choices, are often pre-planned. We choose roles where we can best use our natural skills. It all goes wrong when we find ourselves constantly bored by our jobs; for whatever reason, then we are not fulfilling our 'agreed path'. You will know this when you always get a sense of dread on Monday morning or the minute you put on your work uniform or arrive outside your office building.

Growth of the soul means working with existing skills and learning new ones. Our angels assist in bringing roles that will bring us the greatest joy. Our jobs should use those skills that we would happily exercise for free if money were no object. If you don't feel this delight in your work, it's time to ask the angels to help you to be where you are meant to be.

TAKE THE ANGELS TO WORK

Ask the angels to travel with you on your way to work and stay with you all day. Some jobs can be dangerous, but even if yours isn't you can't have too many angels by your side. Imagine an angel floating along on a cloud above you as you travel in your car or a bus, ride your bike or walk to work.

You can add an angel bumper sticker to your car, stick an angel coin in your handbag or put your work or car keys on an angel key-ring — these will all reaffirm your request. You could also buy yourself a crystal angel figurine to carry with you on work journeys, or to keep somewhere visible at work (see Exercise, opposite).

ANGELS ALL THE WAY

If you take a train or bus to work, you'll find yourself with spare time to fill on the way. If it's safe to do so, then this could be the perfect time to meditate and 'meet your angels' every day on the journey to work. If your journey means that it's not appropriate to close your eyes, maybe this is the time to read your spiritual books, listen to angel music or write your requests and ideas in your angel journal or notebook. Don't waste a single minute!

ANGEL SECRET

Angels long to lead you to successful employment. Watch for their guiding signs. A white feather might be left at the door of your favourite designer boutique – an invitation to look further into fashion as a career choice, perhaps? Does your heart race in excitement as fast as the cars on your local racetrack? Maybe you should consider a career working with cars? Listen for your angel's career signs and feel your answer as your tummy flutters in excitement.

EXERCISE: Boost your career energy

1 Pick up a crystal angel figurine and, using poster putty, attach it to your computer or workspace. During your lunch break, lift off your angel and hold it in your hands, ready to empower it. The angel figurine is a visual representation of the real angel who watches over your working space.

2 As you hold your angel say (or think, if you prefer) the following:

• Crystal angel, I ask for your presence here in my workspace/desk/office. (Fill in the appropriate words here.)

• Please balance the energies around me and bring joy and fulfilment into my work. Allow only positive influences into this space.

• Thank you from all that I am, to all that you are.

Occasionally rinse your crystal angel figurine in fresh clean water and then dry it off with a paper towel. On sunny days you can take your crystal out into the sunlight to 'recharge' it with fresh energies.

ARCHANGEL METATRON: THE ANGEL OF CAREERS

The archangel in charge of careers is Metatron. He is the Angel of the Presence and many call him the greatest of all God's angels. His name is thought to mean 'like God' or 'my name is in him'. He is sometimes seen as a heavenly priest. Some believe Metatron's name itself has magical qualities.

Metatron doesn't have one of the traditional endings to his name such as 'iel' or 'ael'. The name appears to be made from two different Greek words which mean 'after' (to go beyond or transcend) and 'throne'. He is believed to be such a powerful angel because he is seen as the angel who sits next to the throne of God (maybe sitting to write up the records of life – every thought, deed and action of humankind and living souls throughout the Universe). Metatron is particularly good at relationships too, and helps build strong interaction among colleagues, so is important at work.

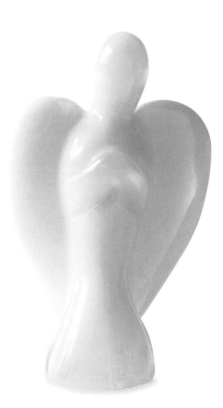

Metatron is recognized in Judaism, Islam and some branches of Christianity. His primary role is keeper of records, the celestial scribe, and he is sometimes seen as a leader or guide. You can ask the Archangel Metatron to help you at work if you want to, or ask him to accompany you during challenging meetings or during changes in your role, when you learn new things.

BUSINESS ANGELS

Metatron works with all types of career, and of course you can always call on the help of your own guardian angel, but many angels are associated with different jobs.

METATRON'S CHARACTERISTICS

- **Appearance:** Metatron is zoften pictured with a writing tablet and quill/pen, and dressed in sumptuousness and opulent clothing.

- **Associated with:** record-keeping, interpersonal relationships, occupations, young people, psychic abilities.

Angel	Career type
Ariel	Jobs that involve animals and birds
Chamuel	Creative jobs such as design, performance, art, building
Gabriel	Communication
Haniel	Mysticism, spirituality
Metatron	Librarianship, book-keeping, writing
Michael	Jobs in administration and accounts, law, creating harmony, counseling
Raguel	Protection, armed forces
Raphael	Healing, nursing, therapy
Raziel	Science, invention
Sariel	Advisory jobs, teaching, training
Uriel	Weather, environment

EXERCISE: Find your perfect career meditation

In this exercise I want to take you straight to your angelic career guidance counsellor. Close your eyes, get comfortable and then we'll begin.

1 First take a number of long, deep breaths. Breathe in through your nose and then blow the breath out through your mouth. In and out, in and out ... blow ... I want you to feel relaxed, very relaxed, and feel all the tension falling away from your body. (You can imagine your angel guide standing behind you blowing away the tension in your body.) You are relaxed and ready for your appointment.

2 Imagine you are walking into a beautiful walk-in wardrobe with big mirrors, well lit and surrounded by rails of clothes. Each set of clothes represents a different type of career choice and with your angel helper you will find the perfect 'fit' for you.

3 Stand in front of the mirror – you look great. Take a deep breath and admire the confident person standing in front of you. Now, with a

wave of his hands, your angel magically places an outfit of clothes upon you. These clothes are perfect for the person doing one of the jobs you are interested in 'trying on'. What are you wearing? What is the job? How does it feel to be wearing these clothes? Are they a good 'fit'?

4 Get a feel for the sensations of wearing these clothes to your new job. Do you feel happy, worried, scared?

5 If you feel comfortable wearing these clothes, then let your angel take you into a trial session at your new job. See yourself doing the job you are interested in, carrying out the actions just as if you were really there. As long as you enjoy the experience, keep going. Who do you meet, and how does it feel to be doing the job you have dreamt about? Does it feel right?

6 Want to try another change of clothes? Go back into the changing room where your angel is ready to 'magic' another set of 'work'

clothes on to your body. Begin the exercise all over again – get a feel for the clothes and the tyoe of career they represent, then see yourself taking on the role at work.

7 Return to the changing room again, if you want to, and repeat the process again.

8 When you're ready, open your eyes and come back into the room. You have brought a lot of insight back with you. Make a few notes about your experience in your angel journal.

Are you clearer on deciding about your dream job now? If not, try the exercise again in a few days. Sometimes people will be standing in the changing room and the angels will surprise them with an outfit for a job they had never considered. If you want to, you can try it this way too – let the angels suggest careers for you. Have fun with your meditation.

ANGEL SECRET

Help the angels in the workplace by being an office angel yourself. Wherever you work, you can bring a little joy to the surroundings of others. Would your boss appreciate a cup of coffee without being asked? Can you work a little later tonight so that the deadline is met? Does a colleague need cheering up? When you go to work today, find a way of bringing a little something extra to your work, or perform a secret 'something' to help a workmate. Ask your angel to inspire you.

ASKING FOR GUIDANCE

Some people feel that, in order to connect with your angels, you need only ask for their help; this is partly true, but hearing their replies is another thing entirely. Your mind needs to be open and relaxed to pick up the 'best advice'.

Here are a few things you can try when asking for guidance:

INFLUENTIAL WATER

Sit next to running water (a stream or river, or even a fountain). Let the sound wash over you and just relax and clear your mind, concentrating only on the sound and sensation of the water as it moves. The continuous sound will take your mind into an altered state of consciousness (a daydreaming state of mind). Your angels will find it easier to reach you when you're relaxed in this way. When you feel a connection, ask your angels your question.

BIBLE DIVINATION

Using a Bible, book of prayers or other religious work, ask your question in your mind and then open the book at random. Ask your angels to guide you to a suitable sentence or paragraph. This is an ancient form of divination (fortune-telling) or oracle. Ask that God sends his angels to guide you on your path or to help with your decisions relating to work and careers.

SLEEP ON IT

Write your question down on a piece of card or pretty paper using a silver or gold marker pen (you can use an ordinary pen but the gold and silver give the whole thing a greater sense of importance or occasion).

Then, when the ink is dry, place the piece of paper or card under your pillow and literally sleep on the problem (you may have to do this several nights in a row). The angels love to bring you answers to your problems in dreams; this might be in symbols or you may be drawn to a certain person or a complete idea, or just hear a few words upon awakening. Stay in tune with your dreams and keep a record of them in your angel journal.

TAKING 'BREAKS'

Although our careers are important to us, it's just as important that we spend time for ourselves, time with family and time on our spiritual and bodily health. Balance is the key in all things and your angel will prompt you if you aren't taking care of all areas. A friend, who was very overwhelmed by her situation at home, suddenly found that she had a sick friend coming to stay, and this was on top of many other problems she was facing in her life. Her friend was overbearing in her demands and ended up staying for much longer than had been agreed. One day my friend had a fall and broke her ankle. She was no longer able to drive her sick friend about and her friend easily made other arrangements, which included helping to take care of her host. The angels had ensured she had her 'break'! This is a dramatic example, but it's much more likely to be something less painful. Do you need a day off work? Maybe the angels will help. Ask for their help.

FINDING YOUR IDEAL JOB

How do you find your perfect job? Working through the list of jobs advertised in your local paper is one way. Visiting a careers adviser or job agency is another way. But do they lead you to the ideal job? Many people don't have a clue about the sort of work they want to do and end up doing work that doesn't fulfil them. In our current world, we live by paying for (most) things using a system of money. Money pays for our homes, food, clothes and medical expenses. We need an income to live.

Do you realize that it's OK to actually love your job? 'Work' doesn't always have to be a chore! Finding a career in an area that you enjoy and are good at is the key to success. Someone once said 'Love what you do and the money will come', and I believe that truly. You can also work for yourself. Success isn't just about earning lots of money – the most important thing is to be fulfilled spiritually.

ANGEL SECRET

Do you have balance in all areas of your life? Ask yourself: 'Have I spent time with my family this week?' 'Have I eaten well and taken care of my body?' 'Have I spent time alone in quiet contemplation, going for a walk or meditating, for example?' Life is not all work and no play. If your work life is taking over, it's time to find ways of making the changes necessary to pull back and renew balance. Give yourself a 'break' or ask your angels to help you.

TRUE LIFE STORY:
AN ANGEL TO WATCH OVER ME

Almost ten years ago, when I lived alone, I went through a stage of being unwell which included dizziness and panic attacks. Sometimes I even blacked out and the doctor thought it might be related to stress. One night I was making my dinner and put the deep-fat fryer on to heat up. While I was waiting, I made myself a cup of tea and sat down to drink it. The next thing I remember is a voice telling me to wake up and to check the chip pan. I ignored it at first because I felt so tired. It was as though I'd been woken up from a dream.

This voice repeated itself again, and again – it was persistent. Eventually I dragged myself up from where I'd passed out on the sofa and went into the kitchen to check on the pan as I'd been instructed. The fryer by this time had started to smoke so I quickly turned it off and realized what a lucky escape I'd had.

I felt so tired that I laid back down on the sofa and when I awoke it was morning and I found myself lying in bed undressed. I always wondered if my Nana had been my angel and saved me from a house fire because I certainly needed the rest. I was very comforted to know that someone was watching over me that day.

EXERCISE: Discover your job skill set

Which things bring you joy? What are you good at? What do you do for free when you have spare time? These are your clues to finding your job skill set.

1 Take your notebook and start a new page (date it). Write at the top of the page: 'All about me'.

2 Then list your perfect skills – imagine your guardian angel is describing you (don't be shy, as no one else will read this). Start each sentence with your name and then add the details: '(Name) is really good at (skill)'. Here are some examples:

• Amanda is really good at cooking

• John is fabulous at painting

• Julie is great at inspiring others

• Ruth has the ability to mend cars on a budget

Make a very long list. I have used different names in the examples, but of course this is just about you and your skills. Start with a list of 40-plus things. Are you good with your hands? Do you enjoy working with animals? Are you creative, well organized, good with people?

3 Now include things that you love or enjoy (start a new page): '(Name) loves/enjoys (fun thing)'. Examples:

• Rachel loves working with animals

• Mo gets excited when she ices cakes in all sorts of great designs

• Dave designs great flowerbeds

• Sian is thrilled when she meets new people

4 Your third list is about what you would love to do but don't do yet. Work in the same way but starting on a fresh page. These may be things that you would love to learn to do or areas you would enjoy exploring in a career. The sky is the limit (or not) – let your fantasy run wild here. '(Name) would love to (anything you would like to learn)'. Examples:

• Pat would love to learn to fly

• Nicola would enjoy speaking French

• Sharon would be excited to work outside

• Victor would be great at woodcarving

Take your time over this. New ideas will appear over the next few days, so add them to the list. Keep going until you feel you have exhausted every option, then work your way through the list. Do any specific jobs come to mind? Are there skills you have or would like to have that might be used in a job of your choice? Is it possible that with help you could create your own job (work for yourself)?

5 Collect together a few favourite sentences (use a highlighter pen to pick them), and then join the sentences together on a new page. At the top of the page, write 'My perfect job', and this time write out a sentence or paragraph as if you were already doing your dream career. Here are two examples:

• I love my work outside with children. I am thrilled that I am using my new ability to speak different languages and travel as part of my work.

• I am really enjoying my career working with animals and writing a book.

Don't judge this in any way, and know that your angels will help it to come about. Your angels bring you signs to fulfil your dreams. Follow up every lead – we are the co-creators of our world. Search for opportunities but keep an open mind. May your future be bright and full of exciting new opportunities.

YOUR DREAM CAREER

Have you ever considered that your dream career might be so much more than just a way of earning a living? Your career could very well be one of the most important reasons for your birth on the planet at this time.

As we've already discussed, our careers define us. They should be a way of displaying the very best of our personal skill set, but many people completely miss the mark. Our need to earn a living and pay the bills get's in the way of us being who we are.

FOLLOW YOUR DREAM

If you ask yourself the question, 'what is my dream job?' Are you able to answer it? Hand the job over to the angels. Write down the question on a slip of paper. Literally write, 'what is my dream job?' or 'how might I best earn my living to incorporate my skills and abilities?'

Then place your question either under your pillow or write up the question in your angel journal. Ask the question before you go to bed at night. Do this for several nights in a row. Write down any 'dreams' or insights you might have from your angels, then follow your dream!

CREATE A CAREER ALTAR

Why not create a career altar on a small table or windowsill to help focus your mind on your intention. Lay a gold shawl or cloth on the top (gold for abundance) and include a happy photograph of yourself. Find a natural pebble or stone with a hole through it (a symbol of a gateway) and place this on your display too. Then add some items to represent your new career, for example:

• A toy car to represent the position of a travelling sales person

• A pot plant to indicate a career working in nature

• An item of jewellery to represent a job in fashion

Don't forget to add an angel figurine to your altar, too. Keep your career altar display fresh and clean and add new items whenever you feel inspired to do so.

'My perfect career makes me feel
excited, contented and useful. I am
working in a role that uses my finest
skills to the best of my abilities.
I visualize myself right now in
my perfect career and my
angels help to guide me.'

ANGELS AND CREATIVITY

'Can you feel my inspiration? I am with you, helping you to build and grow amazing things in your life'

Creativity ... the word immediately inspires us. The angels of creativity are always with us; ask and they will help with all your projects. Open your mind to everything the angels have to offer. Think big – angels will take your projects to a much higher level than you would be brave enough to create on your own. Relax and be inspired! Let your angels lead the way.

THAT FLUTTERING FEELING

When the angels bring you inspirational thought, it drops over your whole body like a net of excitement. You feel it deep within your stomach, just like butterflies. When you get this fluttering feeling, in your stomach you know that the angels are close by. These angels lead you to the perfect materials every time, and the people you need to manifest the ideal outcome.

GET CREATIVE

The angels who work with creativity are also enormous fun. Sometimes it's amusing to create for pleasure only, enjoying the journey rather than the destination. Get out the paints, pencils, crayons, glue and glitter. Can you sew? Use sequins, beads, seeds, crystals or photos. Let your imagination carry you away and ask your angels to help you in making something truly special.

HOMESPUN FUN

It's easy to buy what you need, but how much better it is to make items yourself. Every time you put your own thoughts to work you add a powerful energy to your inventions. It's as if a fairy's wand has sprinkled fairy dust over everything you do. Have fun and set your imagination to work.

CREATIVITY CRYSTALS

If you love crystals then you can certainly work with crystals and creativity. Many people believe that crystals act as a charge to enhance your abilities. They are also very beautiful and inspiring objects in their own right.

The crystals listed in the box below are all suitable to place on your desk, or at your workspace. Some of these crystals are also good for jewellery. Carved crystal angels are always appropriate, but you can use a mixture of tumbled (smooth-edged) stones and naturally shaped pieces.

Crystal	How it can help you
Crystal	Protection, a guardian angel stone
Agate	Perfect for angel communication
Amethyst	Helps with concentration
Citrine	A cluster (pointy) quartz will help shed light on your project
Clear quartz	Grounding and bringing you down to earth
Hematite	Working with the Earth
Jade	A magical stone of otherworldly contact
Lapis lazuli	Place it under your pillow to enhance afterlife
Malachite	Communication
Sodalite	Strengthens contact with your guides and gatekeepers
Tiger's eye	A balancing crystal
Topaz	Psychic protection

EXERCISE: Meditation for inspiration

If you need some inspiration for your creativity, try this meditation on meeting your guardian angel. Play some relaxing music, find a comfortable place to sit and close your eyes.

1 Take a few deep breaths and imagine yourself sitting on a soft, white, fluffy cloud.

2 Feel the cloud take you higher and higher up into the air. You are safe and protected. Your guardian angel is waiting to meet you, way up in the clouds, and now comes floating over to join you.

3 Ask your angel his or her name and hear the name come to you in your mind.

You can ask your angel other questions if you want to, and do spend some time with your angel while you're feeling relaxed. Just float gently on your cloud enjoying your angel's company.

4 When you're ready, say goodbye to your loving guardian angel and know that they will be waiting should you wish to meet up again. Your cloud will bring you slowly and safely down to the ground once more.

5 Allow yourself time to feel grounded. Make a note of your experiences in your journal so that you will remember them.

FUN THINGS TO CREATE

There are lots of different ways to bring the angels into your life. Just remember there is no right or wrong way to do this – just your way. Gather together all the things you need for your project and work in a big space if you can. Ask the angels to sit with you and add their own sparkling magic to your creative projects.

ANGEL SCRAPBOOK

You can buy scrapbooks fairly cheaply from stationery stores, or you can make your own. Staple together some large coloured pages, or use a hole-punch to make holes in the side and fasten your pages together using pretty ribbon. Collect together your angel 'scraps', including angel pictures, quotes and stories, and stick them in your book. You can add glitter, stamps or images cut from Christmas or birthday cards and wrapping paper. Don't waste a single memory of angel experience. Add everything that inspires you and brings you joy.

ANGEL WISH BAGS

Buy or make a small drawstring bag (you can often find these at New Age stores) or use a small zip-up bag. Place a small rose quartz crystal or an amethyst tumbled (smooth-edged) crystal inside. Then write your note or 'wish' to the angels on a piece of paper and fold it up in the bag. The crystal will direct energy to your wish. You can carry this wish bag around with you in your pocket or handbag. If you're lucky enough to come across a tiny angel figurine or angel coin, you could place this inside the bag too. Alternatively, if you prefer, you can fill the bag with angel confetti (pressed silver or gold angel shapes cut from foil; these can be found in specialist gift shops or on the internet).

ANGEL BOX

If you're lucky enough to own an antique box, this is the perfect place to store all your magical angel items. Alternatively, make your own box by decorating an old shoebox, or similar, with wrapping paper or wallpaper. Maybe you have a pretty hat box you could use for this. Place a lacy scarf inside to use as a 'tablecloth' and collect an angel figure and some magical crystals. Then, when you're ready to meditate with your angels, place the cloth over the box and display your angel items on the top. Afterwards you can put everything away safely. Your angel box is also the perfect place to store your magical items. What craft skills can you use to make it even more special? If it's a wooden box, carve the word 'ANGELS' on the top. Cut out letters from magazines, stick

them on to the box and then cover it with clear varnish. Sew patchwork fabric, quilted or appliqué angels cut from cloth on to another fabric and use this to cover or line your box. There are many possibilities for making your angel box special.

ANGEL PROTECTION CARDS

Using the backs of old Christmas cards or some lightweight card bought from a stationery store, stick a photo of your loved ones in the middle. Then write the words 'Angels protect me' above the photo and decorate the outside with pictures of angels (you can draw or stick them on). You could make one card for each member of your family. How about hanging the cards from

---

ANGEL SECRET

Your angels are full of ideas, so let them inspire you. Can't feel them close? Sit for a few moments, in an outdoor space if possible. Close your eyes and ask the angels to surround your body and flood your aura (energy field) with their loving light. Sit for a while and enjoy this sensation. When the energy stops flowing and you feel you have had your fill, open your eyes and begin work.

some thread in a type of mobile, popping them into photo grippers, or just tucking them into the side of a bedroom mirror?

ANGEL CANDLEHOLDER

Find a small, low-sided jar (or glass tumbler) and wash and dry it. Paste an angel sticker, angel confetti shapes or angel images on the outside (for safety's sake, don't add anything to the inside), and add some pretty glitter glue or glitter shapes so that they catch the light. Leave to dry. (You can also decorate plant pots in the same way.) If you really want some fun, use glass paints. Draw a simple image on a piece of paper and place this on the inside of the jar. Use it as a template to outline the shape on the outside using special outlining glass paints. When the outline is dry, fill it in with colours so that it looks like a stained-glass window. Remove the paper. What a wonderful present you could make for an angel fan! Your glass candleholder is ideal for the small candles in metal holders known as tea-lights. Place a tea-light inside the holder and light it.

ANGEL DOLLS

Why not make your own angels? You just need a doll (or teddy bear), some scraps of fabric (lace, netting, etc), sequins and some silver and gold thread. You can use templates for dolls' clothing (found at sewing shops) or find a doll with an outfit you can copy or adapt. Don't forget to add some wings! My local garden centre sells mini feather wings to hang on your Christmas tree, but you could very easily make some out of fabric or netting. If you are making these dolls for young children, make sure they are completely safe and that there are no loose parts (or small items that might fall away and cause a choking hazard).

ANGEL DIARY

Make a note of the angel experiences in your own life by recording them in your diary. You can make up your own code by drawing a little feather on the pages where you have found feather gifts, a star when something magical has happened, a candle when someone has brought a little light into your life, and so on. The more you record your experiences, the more things will happen.

MAGICAL OUTDOOR ANGEL SPACE

Can you beg, steal or borrow the corner of a garden or a yard? If so, you can make yourself a magical outdoor angel space. You will need a seat where you can meditate – this might be a log or a fold-out garden chair. Decorate your space with outdoor lights, wind chimes and natural objects that you find around you. Add a few angel figurines and plant some scented flowers. This is the perfect place for you to sit and talk to your angels.

ANGEL WEBSITE

Learn how to build a website and dedicate it to the angels. It's not as difficult as it looks. You can write about your own angel experiences, list your favourite angel books, and add lots of angel pictures and information. Then, when you have finished, ask people with other angel websites if they will link with you so that you can all enjoy each other's hard work. A website is a great way of letting your angelic personality shine, and you can constantly add to it. You could try some of the following:

• Search the internet for free angel clip art (angel images) you can use to illustrate your site.

• Ask your new friends to share their angel tips.

• Share your angel prayers, poems and artwork.

COLOUR AND ANGELS

Many people regularly like to change their hair colour, their clothes and their whole look. What works one day doesn't necessarily work the next. We adjust the paint colours on our walls and the make-up colours on our faces. Our bodies respond to different colours on different days.

If you are someone who changes their clothes several times a day, then maybe your aura (your body's energy field) changes colour frequently too. Angels also work with different colours. Which colour do you 'feel' right now? This angel might stay with you for several days or even change several times during the day. Look up your colour angel on the chart below.

Colour	Angel	Qualities and uses
Silver	Ariel	Silver is the colour of money and the moon. Ariel usually works with nature, so this is the perfect day to spend outside – weather permitting. You are feeling especially magical today. I bet a full moon isn't far away!
White	Uriel	White is the sign of purity and peace. Today might be the perfect time to create order in your life or just spend some quiet time alone. Uriel will help you find the perfect spot.
Yellow	Sandalphon	Yellow is the colour of fun. If you are in a yellow mood, you are probably enjoying great vitality right now. If you don't feel as yellow as you would like to be, make sure you eat healthily today and the yellow brightness in your aura will shine. Ask Sandalphon to help.
Black	Michael	We sometimes say that a person is negative if they have a black aura around them, but Michael uses black to banish negativity and balance your aura. The colour black is also used by Michael for protection.

Colour	Angel	Qualities and uses
Brown	Chamuel	Today your world is full of joy and happiness. Brown is the colour of earth, which means you are feeling very grounded and 'together'. Chamuel is helping you see the beauty of life around you.
Blue	Raphael	Feeling blue? It doesn't necessarily mean you're ill, but you might need the help of the angel healer Raphael to bring your colours into alignment. Sit back and relax while Raphael goes to work.
Green	Metatron	Green with envy? Maybe, but this colour is also used to represent fertility and new growth. Metatron will use this colour to bring about good luck and fortune today.
Gold	Gabriel	Gold is often a colour used to represent money, but it also shows abundance or 'good wealth'. Gold is the colour of the sun in magical terms, so Gabriel will use this colour to bring some light into your life.
Lilac	Haniel	Lilac is the colour of magical meditations, and is also used to indicate wisdom and knowing. Haniel will work this colour on your inner strengths, including knowledge and understanding.
Orange	Raguel	Orange is the colour of happiness and joy. How can you feel sad with this colour in your aura? Many children work with this colour, so if you are having an orange day Raguel will be reminding you of your inner child and how to bring plenty of fun into your life today.
Pink	Jophiel	Pink is the colour of unconditional love. This might be the love you have for your friends, your family or even your pets. Are you 'in the pink'? Jophiel will be showing you that you are at peak fitness and full of inner calm.
Purple	Sariel	Purple is a very spiritual colour. Today you may be concentrating on developing your psychic gifts or just being open to your natural intuition. Sariel will guide you. It's the perfect day to look for new magical reading material.
Red	Azrael	Some might be red with anger or jealousy, but you might just be full of passion and lust! Red can represent romantic relationships too. Azrael will help keep this colour in balance today.

ANGELS AND FRIENDSHIP

'I am your friend, your companion, and am always at your side as your longest-serving, dearest love'

Your guardian angel is your closest friend. Your angel loves you totally, unconditionally, never judging, always wanting for you exactly what you want for yourself. Loneliness is not being alone – you are never alone. Loneliness means you are disconnected from those around you, and from your guardian angel.

Friendship with your angel means respect, honour, understanding and truth. Hiding or pretending with your guardian angel is pointless – your angel already knows everything there is to know about you right now and loves you exactly as you are. Spirit forms communicate mainly using telepathy. They already know the truth about how you feel inside. Practise communicating with your loved ones by being honest about how you feel. You should be polite and gentle, and it takes time for people to get used to this change. As human souls we are evolving so that our inner thoughts are becoming more transparent anyway; once we make the transition as spirits at the end of our physical life we too will communicate like this all the time. Start now!

ANGEL SECRET

Smiling creates a chemical change in the body and helps us to feel so much better about ourselves and everyone around us. Use this wonderful gift to change the lives of others in a simple way that has no cost on your time. Ask your angels to help you get started. Smile at your local shopkeeper or the lady at the bus stop. They will notice the change in your aura. You will feel better too. Everybody benefits.

EXERCISE: Meet your guardian angel – Meditation 2

Meditation is a wonderful way to meet up with your best friend, your guardian angel. When you are in a gently relaxed mutative state, your angel can reach out to you. Each time you do this exercise, the meditation becomes stronger. Practice is the key.

1 Find a comfortable place to relax. Support your back if you need to and check that the temperature of the room is restful, but not so warm that you fall asleep. If you wish, you can do the full relaxation exercise described on pages xx–xx.

2 Close your eyes and take some deep breaths. Breathe in deeply through your nose and blow the breath out through your mouth. Do this three or four times, then breathe normally in and out.

3 Relax your shoulders, neck and head, then your arms, back, tummy and legs. Relax, relax.

4 Imagine the warmth of a gentle sun shining down upon you, the birds singing in the trees, the leaves rustling gently in the breeze. All the while you are becoming more and more relaxed.

5 In the distance you can hear the sound of a beautiful choir of harmonious voices singing together; the voices are calling to you. Begin to feel the pull and gently float towards the sound of the voices. Float along gently, safely, feeling more and more relaxed. Hear the beautiful voices, the sound of the angels' singing, breathtaking, perfect, peaceful.

6 In the distance, you see a white marble structure with four columns. Angels stand all around and the light is split into many rainbow colours. As you get closer, you notice a soft white seating area in the centre, like a giant beanbag, waiting for you to sink comfortably into the middle. The large cushion takes your weight perfectly and moulds to fit your shape, holding you completely. You feel weightless, supported, relaxed.

7 The angels indicate to you that you should lie back

and enjoy the sounds they are producing, and you do so, feeling ever more relaxed, relaxed.

8 Then the music becomes quieter and you open your eyes. You can feel the change and wait in anticipation as your own dear guardian angel steps forward, bringing the feeling of total unconditional love. Your angel indicates that you should remain in this laid-back, relaxed position and asks you to observe. You may now begin to ask the following questions:

- Are you male or female? (although without gender, angels often choose to show themselves in one form or another)

- What is your name? (your angel may give you the name of a traditional angel, a common name or a name you have never heard before)

- How do we work together? (you can request specific signs at this time if you wish)

Now ask specific questions about things that are currently troubling you, such as your health, work or relationships.

9 When you're ready, indicate this to your angel and they will begin to withdraw, smiling, happy. Your angel is here waiting for you at any time. It's time to return.

10 Now you find you are lifting up from your relaxing position and beginning to float back to your starting position ... back, back, back. Can you hear the birds singing again, can you feel the breeze through the trees, the warmth of the sun?

11 As soon as you are ready, open your eyes and come back into the room. Awake, awake, awake. Don't worry, you won't get lost – although you could easily fall asleep, so make sure that you set an alarm if you have to go to work. Write down your experiences in your angel notebook so you can remember anything important, or recall important insights you gained during your meditation experience. Sometimes you don't know what's important until a later date.

ANGELS IN REAL LIFE

Angels appear in many different ways in dreams, visions and meditations, but they also appear in real life. It's common for people to be in a life-threatening situation where a stranger appears to help and then disappears without a trace. When describing the stranger later, each person may have seen something, or someone, completely different. Real-life angels may wear unusual clothes or mismatched clothes (summer and winter items all jumbled up) or maybe clothes that seem out of date for the time period as if they don't understand what would be appropriate for today. These little clues seem to give them away. Other common features are piercing blue eyes and white or blonde hair. The angel might be very tall, but not always. The energy of the 'person' is usually the ultimate giveaway – they just feel different, very loving, kind and peaceful. Have you seen an angel in real life?

TRUE LIFE STORY:
ENCOUNTER WITH AN ANGEL?

I was in town one day and for some reason I looked up and noticed this man. As he walked past me I smiled and he smiled at me – nothing unusual, except at first I thought he was a tramp or a traveller, but he was clean and just dressed in this bizarre long coat. When I smiled at him he looked straight into my eyes and he had the most piercing blue eyes that were filled with kindness and love. At that moment I truly felt as if I had looked into the eyes of God. I don't know where that feeling or thought came from but it was so strong that I wanted to turn round and see if the man was still walking but I couldn't.

I know it's stupid but I just knew he would be gone. This experience has stayed clearly in my mind and I can still see and feel his eyes and the kindness and love from them. I always wondered, 'Could he have been an angel?' I know that feeling was overwhelming and I knew in my heart I had looked into the eyes of something not from our world.

MAKING GOOD FRIENDS

We can never have enough friends. Ask your angel to help you find suitable people for friendship. Most people have friends for different reasons. There is the friend you meet for coffee, the friend you always go clubbing with and the friend who looks after your cat when you go on holiday. Friendship is about mutual respect and shared intimate conversation. It helps a lot if you have something in common.

WHAT MAKES A GOOD FRIEND?

Remember that your guardian angel is your best friend. What do you need from your guardian angel? Use these same attributes with your own earthly friends. Write a list. What sort of words might you include on your 'good friend list' – loving, patient, non-judgemental? What do you want from your friendship? A good friend is someone you can trust and know will always tell you the truth. A good friend cares about you and their ultimate goal is to ensure they are there for you in your time of need – that means you have to consider this as your goal too.

Friendship is giving and taking – when one side of the partnership is always doing the listening and the other is always doing the talking, the balance of scales is uneven. It puts great strain on your relationship.

MAKE IT WORK

Do you have friendships that drain you? Talk about your feelings and see if you can create a healthier and more balanced relationship. You never know, your friend may be feeling exactly the same way. If you value your friendship, it is worth sitting down and talking about what it is that keeps it from working. And if you can't resolve your differences, you may just have to agree between you that the relationship is not working.

ANGEL SECRET

Angels like to perform many of their acts of kindness in secret, and you can too. Find a way of helping someone anonymously – the mystery is magical in itself. Be a secret friend.

EXERCISE: Make a friendship altar

1 Using a small coffee table (a round one is particularly appropriate), lay a yellow or multi-coloured cloth over the top. Cut out some pictures of happy, smiling faces from magazines.

You also need a photograph of yourself. Cut out a piece of cardboard the same size as an empty photo frame (the larger the better).

2 Stick the photo of yourself in the middle and add the smiley people all around the photo. These images represent friends, so look for many faces of different types including multi-ethnic, both sexes and all ages.

3 Put the photo montage in the frame and place it in the centre of your table. Place an angel figurine to watch over the display and add a selection of crystals to charge up the energy ready to put it to work.

4 Say the following words or make up some of your own: I am a loving, willing friend, angels. I welcome new people into my life for fun and happy relationships based on mutual respect; friends for fun, friends for sports, creative pastimes and friends to talk to in times of need. I offer myself in return as a good friend. With God's will, let it be so.

5 If you want, you can add photos of current friends in pretty frames to your display. You can use old photos at first, and take the opportunity of contacting some old friends if the photos make you feel that you miss them.

6 Push your altar table up against the wall and hang some friendship photos (see below) on the wall behind the table.

7 Create large montages of yourself and others riding bikes, dancing, walking your dog, taking part in sporting activities, dressing up for fancy dress parties and taking part in all sorts of new activities. You will soon be able to replace the faces of strangers with images of your real friends, both old and new.

TAKING FRIENDSHIP PHOTOS

If you don't have any photos of your friends for your altar, maybe now is the time to take some. Arrange some fun events with your existing friends. Warn everyone in advance that you want to take photos of you all having fun. Everyone will be excited at the opportunity of getting together. Send out official invitations if you wish – even if it's just to tell everyone to meet up at a local bar. Arrange a theme to mark the occasion.

Here are a few suggestions for themed nights:

• Bring a photo of yourself as a baby

• Wear pink

• Bring a new friend

• Wear a hat

• Bring a wrapped present for one of your friends (set a low ceiling price)

• Knit or crochet a square for a blanket (teach your friends to knit or crochet if they don't know how); this may take several nights so include an evening when you stitch all the squares together and donate the blanket to a charity.

• Bring old clothes you no longer want (put up a big rail, put shoes in a row, display handbags and jewellery on a table). Put a small price tag on each item and donate the money to charity at the end (someone can volunteer to take everything that's left unsold to a charity shop).

All these things just break the ice and get the event going. Organize different types of activities – go out for dinner, arrange friends' birthday parties, try new activities, and so on. Just organizing the events will help to create new friends as you encourage your existing friends to bring along others. Perhaps you can organize charity fundraising activities; every couple of months a new person organizes the next activity. But don't forget to take lots of photos to place on your friendship altar!

FRIENDSHIP ANGEL STONE

If you're going to be separated from a good friend for any length of time, why not exchange small gifts with each other? Go for a walk together and collect some small rounded pebbles (stones with no sharp edges that are large enough to draw or paint on but not so large that they are too heavy to carry).

Then sit down with a collection of paints (acrylic paints are good) or felt-tip pens and have some fun. Draw little angel figures or stars (full of power) and then colour them in. Yellow is a great colour for friendship, but create something that has meaning for you both.

After your craft is dry, exchange your angel pebble gifts with each other. Now you have a reminder of your friendship to carry with you, and the stones are infused with each of your energies.

RECEIVING MESSAGES FROM YOUR ANGEL FRIENDS

Always be ready to experience loving messages from your guardian angel friends. These messages may come in many different ways, so keep your eyes and ears open for contact. Maybe your angel will reach you in one of the following ways:

- You may hear words from a human friend whose message has a deeper meaning for you than even they are aware of.

- You may interpret words on a TV or radio programme as a message.

- There may be a phrase that jumps out at you from a book or magazine.

- An overheard private conversation in which there are 'messages' that have special meaning for you.

- You may see signs on posters or words that jump out from car registration plates.

- Birds, butterflies, dragonflies or other creatures acting in unusual ways may have a significance for you, especially if they seem particularly friendly.

OTHER-SIDE FRIENDS

Angels are the ultimate friends when they are waiting to collect us once this life is over. Angels escort us from one side to the other and take our hands as we pass through the gate of Heaven.

SEEING ANGELS

There are many thousands of documented cases of people seeing angels when they are sick, during operations and when they are unconscious. Angels appear to comfort those whose body is in physical trauma. Of course, these people don't die but, instead, come back into their physical bodies to tell us their tales of angel encounters.

Angels have been known to tell the person 'Go back now, it's not your time', meaning 'this is not your time to die'. Angels are often the ones who push your spirit body back into your physical body, sending you back to Earth to continue your physical life for more years to come.

WORKING WITH THE GRIEVING AND DYING

Families of the dying, and health-care professionals who spend time with those near the end of their life, will occasionally see glimpses of these other realms. It's quite common for the sick to see loved ones who have passed over in those final days and hours, nearly always accompanied by angels, of course. Patients report these experiences to their nurses, and the nurses can sometimes see these amazing sights too – that's a real privilege. Other angel-related experiences include smelling the wonderful scent of roses and hearing angelic, choir-type music.

Seeing loved ones who have already crossed to the Heaven side doesn't mean you too are going to die. They often appear to reassure us that everything is going to be OK and that we will recover.

Those close to their 'time' may see a light at the end of a tunnel. When passing over, they are drawn to this light and all the beautiful feelings that go with it. Heaven is a wonderful place of love and this is where our angels reside.

TRUE LIFE STORY: **THE CROW**

I was very close to my Gran, who actually brought me up. When I was little she used to tease me and say that when she died she wanted to come back as a big black crow and if we saw her at the window we were to throw her out some bread. We all used to laugh at her and I used to reply that if I was coming back I'd rather be something other than a crow!

Well, this all happened over 30 years ago. Sadly, my Gran died six months after my daughter was born. Five years later it was my daughter's first school trip. She came and got into bed beside me for about an hour before it was time to get up and get ready for the trip.

I was making her breakfast and told her to go into her room and get her things ready but she immediately came running out of the room, saying 'There's a bird in my bedroom'. I went to look and I'm a bit scared of birds so I was stunned when I saw what was sitting on her wardrobe – a huge, black crow! I let out a yell but it just sat there looking at me. All the windows and doors were closed, but, having said that, there was a fireplace in the bedroom where maybe a small bird could have came down the chimney – but this crow was huge and there was not a speck of soot anywhere in the room.

The crow didn't move at all. It just sat there. In the end I called a neighbour round and he came in to help. Even when he went into the room to get it, the crow didn't fly about and he was able to lift it up and carry it outside. It just looked at us and then flew away.

When I went to visit my mother and my grandfather, I told them about the experience and they both said: 'Don't worry, it was your Gran. She always said she would come back as a big black crow and you know she would not have missed your daughter's very first school trip.'

'My angel is my greatest friend. I am always supported and loved'

ANGELS AND HEALING

'I bring you positive health and well-being, and continually work on uplifting your energy to the highest levels'

Our bodies are amazing vessels for the soul. Our human forms are an extraordinary gift on loan during our earthly visit. Your body was chosen to enable you to learn the lessons you best needed for your short time on this planet.

Our job on Earth is to take care of our bodies to the best of our abilities. Health is important but looks are not. Thousands of pounds are spent on cosmetics, hair products and fashion each year. The angels despair at our vanity but they long to help us.

The angels of healing concentrate on the health of our physical bodies, cleaning and clearing from the inside out. They lead us to better choices but, as with all angelic 'advice', we can choose to listen – or not. Remember, then, the important lesson is always health first. What have you done to take care of your own body today?

TRUE LIFE STORY:
THE HEALING ROSE

Sally was a nurse. One day she went to the home of an elderly lady to give her a flu jab. The woman was upset after losing her husband a few weeks before and Sally felt great compassion for the woman. Sally leant down to give her a cuddle to cheer her up, and as she stood up again she felt an incredible sense of warmth and love starting from her toes and moving up through her whole body. Sally knew she wasn't the only person hugging the patient that day. Then she saw a rose appear in her mind's eye – what was it for? She asked the woman 'What's your favourite flower?' and, of course, the answer was 'A rose'!

HEALING WITH THE ANGELS

Jesus was the master healer. He understood how to work with universal energy to bring about healing using positive thought. Most parents do this instinctively too. If a child falls over and hurts themselves, it's only natural to hug them close to comfort them. When a colleague is in trouble, we lay a hand on their shoulder. When a youngster is frightened, we offer a hand in friendship. When a lover is sad, we may draw their head close to ours.

Healing is a natural thing among humans and many of the children born into our New Age are even better at this ancient skill than their elders. They work with the universal healing energy from very early on in life and understand that our 'intent' forms the power behind the healing.

We heal through the power of our will and positive thought.

HEALING PRACTICES

Many formal types of healing are used around the world, including spiritual healing and Reiki (pronounced 'ray-key'). Reiki is an ancient Japanese system devised by Dr Mikao Usui. Each system uses the same base energy known as Chi (also called Qi, Prana or 'life force energy').

Many healers call in angels or healing figures to assist them. A Reiki healer would probably ask for the assistance of Dr Usui, their own guardian angel and the other person's guardian angel. You can also ask for the help of the Archangel Raphael, the healing angel, if you want to give this a go.

If you are far away from home or walking up a mountainside, for

> ## ANGEL SECRET
>
> The angels can communicate more easily when we are around water. Take a walk along a riverbank, take a rowing boat out into the middle of a lake or swim in the sea. If you are not close to a natural source of water, you can take a bath or shower as this works equally well. Ask your angels to communicate with you while you relax.

example, energy healing may well be useful to ease any pain you are suffering. Of course, you hear many extraordinary claims for this type of healing and I have no doubt that these stories are true.

MY EXPERIENCE

I remember sitting on a train with toothache. I had no pain-killers with me and there was no one else in the carriage. I asked angels to help me with the spiritual practice of Reiki healing and it worked, taking away the pain until I could get home and receive treatment. It was wonderful to feel the pain relief, but ultimately I still needed treatment for the tooth.

HEALTH WARNING

Take note: Any healing system that works like this is called 'complementary' for a reason. 'Complementary' healing should be used alongside your traditional doctor's advice (don't stop taking pills, for example, without the explicit instructions of your doctor).

Spiritual healing is just an 'extra' and can be useful while waiting for other help to arrive. If necessary, with any pain, do ensure you seek professional help to get the problem properly diagnosed. Pain is there for a reason – it lets you know there is a problem with your body.

TRUE LIFE STORY:
TAKING THE PAIN AWAY

I have severe IBS which leaves my stomach bloated and in pain. One night about three weeks ago I had the most horrendous stomach pain. It was so bad that the pain had actually woken me. I decided to ask for the healing angels to take the pain away. Immediately I saw seven figures in the corner of our bedroom near the window. They were all in a line one behind another. The one at the front was purple and violet in colour and the others were white and they were very tall – around seven foot.

The vision only lasted for a few minutes and I wasn't scared at all. Seeing these angelic beings really relaxed me and I soon fell into deep sleep. When I woke up I was pain-free, but the vision is still as vivid now as it was then and I know these angels were real.

PSYCHIC PAIN

Sometimes in life it's possible literally to feel the pain of others. This works on a higher psychic level, particularly between twins and between a parent and his or her children. No doubt these experiences are a carry-over from a previous time when humans relied more on instinct.

I've discovered that many children born today have these abilities from birth. To feel the emotions of others in a kind of 'sixth sense' is a natural ability, an angelic gift.

ANGEL SECRET

There are angels – like Archangel Raphael (see pages 112–113) – who can help with pain control. If you want your guardian angels to help with your own pain or suffering, simply close your eyes, take a few deep breaths, and relax. Then, when you are ready, ask your angels for help.

EXERCISE: Heal your headache

Draw on your own natural healing abilities to work on yourself next time you have a headache. Many headaches are caused by dehydration or eye problems, so make sure you are not ignoring these body warnings, which need treating right away. The technique that follows is particularly useful for a stress headache.

1 Sit quietly, with your back against a wall if possible (this will help you feel more secure and relaxed).

2 Place the palms of your hands over your eyes.

Imagine your angel standing behind you with hands on each shoulder. Feel their healing light energy pouring down into your own body and into your hands.

3 Imagine that healing energy is now flooding into your own body and 'washing away' the pain (particularly focus on the source of the pain caused by your headache). All the while try to relax as much as possible.

Afterwards, remember to thank your angel.

TRUE LIFE STORY:
TAKE YOUR TABLETS

When my Dad was alive I always knew when he was not well. It didn't matter where I was at the time, or what time it was, I always knew. Dad had a bad heart and if he was getting pains in his chest I always felt pains in my chest too. I always phoned my Mum or, if I was close by at the time, I went round and told him to take his heart medication.

About ten minutes after he took his medication all my pains went and so did his. Sadly, one night I had this terrible pain in my chest that woke me up. It was really bad and I thought of my Dad immediately. I had this terrible feeling come over me. I was very scared and felt sick. It seemed like someone had died and I just couldn't settle. In the end I phoned my Mum. It was 3.50 a.m. and she was not very happy to get woken at that time as my Dad was fast asleep. She said if I was so worried maybe I should get the doctor to check me out. Confused, I got back into bed.

Moments later my phone rang and sadly it was my mother-in-law telling me my father-in-law had just passed away.

ARCHANGEL RAPHAEL

Archangel Raphael is the healing angel. Paintings of Raphael often show him walking with a caduceus, which is a staff entwined by two snakes; occasionally the staff has wings at the top. The caduceus is often used as a symbol for medicine (although traditionally this would be the 'rod of Asclepius' which has a single snake and no wings).

Raphael's name means 'God heals' or 'healer of God'. He is an angel found in Christianity, Islam and Judaism and the Guardian of the Tree of Life. Rophe (from the modern Hebrew) also means 'doctor of medicine'.

RAPHAEL'S CHARACTERISTICS

- **Appearance:** carries a staff, bottle or flask, points Heavenward using his right forefinger.

- **Associated with:** dispensing chemists/pharmacies, the blind, lovers, nurses, shepherds, travellers, the young, therapists.

- **Celebrations:** feast days – 29 September and 24 October; patron saint of medical workers (Catholic).

ANGEL HEALING CARDS

The Archangel Raphael appears on many gifts (such as angel coins or mini figurines) that you can carry around with you in your pocket or bag. Why not make something of your own?

Many stationery stores sell business card-sized cardboard cut-outs ready for you to create your own stationery. You can use these to create your own angel healing card, perfect for keeping in your purse or wallet. Christmas cards with angel pictures on the front are also perfect.

Use an old credit card as a template and draw round the shape, cutting it out to the perfect size. On the reverse of the card, write or print one of the following wishes:

RAPHAEL
Angel of healing
May the owner of this card
always stay fit and well
With grateful thanks

RAPHAEL
Angel of healing
May the owner of this card
Always be filled with your
healing light
With grateful thanks

HEALING CARDS FOR OTHERS

Why not make several cards and give them away as gifts? You can print them off using your computer; then, to illustrate the reverse side, cut out images from magazines and stick them on, draw or paint your own, or use stickers. You could keep one in your gym bag, one inside your desk and another in your car.

EXERCISE: Angel healing triangle meditation

1 Close your eyes and relax. Take several deep breaths and circle your shoulders around. Shake out your arms and legs a little to loosen up. Sit in a comfortable spot and begin your visualization.

2 Imagine three awesome and powerful healing angels standing around you creating a healing triangle above your head with their arms outstretched and touching. You are sitting underneath their hands and surrounded by protective, healing wings.

3 Pouring from their hands is a surge of blue and gold healing energy. This healing energy sparkles with life – feel it as it surrounds your body, washing away any impurities, tensions and disease (dis-ease) in your outer energy body. Spend as long as you need on this exercise (maybe 10–20 minutes).

4 Imagine the healing energy is cleansing and clearing all toxins from your body. Let the angels wash them away with the power of the blue and golden light. When you're ready, the angels will stop the flow and enfold you in their wings for a healing hug. Feel the loving healing pouring from your healing angels. When you're finished, open your eyes, and smile!

EXERCISE: Create a healing angel altar

Does someone in your family need a little extra help in the healing department? If so, you can make a healing altar for them. To do this you will need:

• A photo or photos of the person who needs the healing. If you don't have a photo of the person where they look happy and relaxed, use something to represent the person (an item belonging to them would be perfect, such as a piece of jewellery, scarf, glove or tie).

• An altar cloth – if you can find something in blue or gold this would be perfect, but white is a suitable alternative. Things you can use include a pillowcase, tablecloth or silky scarf, as long as it is big enough to cover your table or shelf.

• A candle – scented candles can be wonderful, but for best effect make sure you use ones scented by natural fragrances. Use a blue or gold candle if you can find one. Rosemary and eucalyptus are ideal, but lavender and rose are good substitutes.

• An angel figurine, angel coin or angel picture.

• A clear quartz crystal (any size).

• A vase of fresh white flowers or a single flower in a vase. It would also be appropriate to use a flowering pot plant with white flowers.

1 Place your cloth on a table, worktop, cupboard or shelf. Display your items on the top and light the candle. Say the following: Healing angels, with your will and the highest good of all, I request healing energy for … (insert name of person). Shine your light into the heart of this person, restoring them to their best possible health, with loving thanks. (Add your own name here if you want to.)

2 Sit in quiet meditation and relaxation for a while. Hold the image of your loved one being healed by the angels.

3 When you feel it's the appropriate time (after around ten minutes or so), blow out the candle. Never leave the candle burning alone in a room. If you're working or reading in the space, and can keep an eye on the candle, you can leave it burning a little while longer.

THE ILL AND THE DYING

Nurses, doctors and those who work with the sick and the dying often see angels. Angels watch over the dying and over newborn babies. They take care of our physical healing and work with us when we are in altered states of consciousness (in a coma, for example).

It has been known for people to wake up after a major hospital operation and share miraculous stories of seeing their guardian angels whom they have met 'visually' for the first time when unconscious.

Angels tell us, their charges, how they watch over us, and even push us back into our bodies when it's not 'our time' to cross over to the other side. Who is the mystery figure that walks the hospital wards at night? Why, it's an angel, of course!

SEMI-CONSCIOUSNESS

When we suffer long-term illnesses, or are in hospital, fading in and out of consciousness, we are actually more likely to see our guardian angels than at any other time.

Your angel may appear as a human type of guide or as a white-gowned, glowing figure with wings. Your angel may whisper words of comfort to you

TRUE LIFE STORY:
THE HEADACHE ANGEL

One day my Mum was really in pain with a bad head and I offered to give her some healing. I held my hands over her neck and shoulder area and something caught my eye. I saw a great angel and I knew immediately it was the Archangel Michael. He was really tall and standing in front of my Mum. He had a sword and, just as when a king knights someone, I saw the angel doing a similar action, first on to Mum's left shoulder and then her right.

The angel stayed with us for ages and then disappeared shortly after I had finished. I had such a clear image of his sword that I drew it afterwards. I still have the drawing.

or just place a healing hand in your hand. Whether you see your angel or not, just know that they are always with you during your hours of need.

SPIRITUAL AWARENESS

When my own father had been in hospital for many weeks in a coma, I longed to be able to sit with him during the night. One night I asked my angels if I could stay with him as I drifted off to sleep. In the morning when I woke up I could still feel my father's hand in my hand and knew that on some level my spirit had stayed at the hospital while I slept at home in bed. Thanks, angels!

ANGEL SECRET

It's OK to ask the angels to take care of someone in hospital. The secret is to ask your guardian angel to ask the person's angels to watch over them. We have to make sure not to interfere with someone's life plan (sometimes being sick has been 'chosen' to help learn lessons on earth), so after your request always say 'if it be in accordance with the will of (the person's name) for their divine plan and highest good'.

ANGEL PIN HEALING

When you're visiting someone in hospital, attach an angel pin to their sponge bag or robe (make sure you tell them it's there). Ask the angels to use this little symbol as an indication that you are asking for healing.

Make sure your pin or button is age-appropriate (don't place something small near the possessions of a young child where it might create a choking hazard). Some manufacturers create soft toys (usually teddy bears) with wings and some of these are suitable for young children. An angel-bear might be an appropriate gift for a youngster in hospital (make sure the child's name is written on the label).

ANGEL SECRET

Angels can help other people in pain too, if it's appropriate for their personal growth and journey. If you spot an ambulance, see an accident or notice someone in pain, it's OK to ask your guardian angel to send over appropriate healing and pain relief. If you're lucky, you may even see the angels at work!

TRUE LIFE STORY:
HEALING ANGELS?

I had a beautiful experience at a healing weekend in Somerset. I was in a group doing a healing meditation and our teacher gave us a visualization where we were being lifted higher and higher. All of a sudden I saw in my mind's eye a pillar of beautiful light (this is how I see angels, along with the feeling of enormous, overwhelming love and warmth). The angel was holding a goblet that contained golden liquid, which he poured into my mouth, and as it went down my throat it was warm and soothing. I felt it go all the way down into my heart and stay there, completely covering and protecting it. Strangely, I'd been having trouble with my throat for a while but maybe it was a spiritual rather than a physical problem. .

EXERCISE: Self-healing meditation

If you're feeling a little unwell, try this meditation, which may help you feel better.

1 Lie down on your bed. Close your eyes and imagine the angels standing above you with a healing pillar of light. The light starts at your head and moves slowly down through your body to your feet. Take as long as you wish on this exercise. Enjoy the warmth of the light and the relaxed, loving feeling it gives you.

2 You may fall asleep if you're already a little tired and weary from the day. This isn't a problem and won't stop the meditation from working at all. (Set your alarm if you need to be up by a certain time.)

3 As soon as you're ready, gently sit up and open your eyes. Write down any experiences you may have in your journal. You may need a refreshing hot drink to wake you back up again. Enjoy!

PASSING OVER

Sometimes the most appropriate form of healing is for the angels to be present when the sick are passing over. It might be that soul's 'time' or the body may be too ill to continue life in a happy and comfortable way. That is when the best possible outcome is to ask the angels to escort your loved one to the other side.

THE RIGHT TIME

Don't worry – if it's not their time the angels won't take them away (it won't be your fault if they choose to cross over, and you can't make this happen just by thinking or wishing). Often the dying see their angels and maybe a deceased loved one when their final moments come. What a comfort it must be to know not only that the angels are exactly where they are meant to be but also that your loved one knows they are there.

The crossing-over angel is called Azrael, the 'Angel of Death'. This loving angel is often the first being people see as their soul leaves the physical body for the last time before their journey to the afterlife. Azrael is rarely alone. He brings along the soul's guardian angel, and often excited relatives on the other side of life will also journey into our realms to escort the dying person over.

HEALING IN THE AFTERLIFE

Any illnesses and disabilities of the physical body no longer exist in the spiritual body. Once the soul crosses to the other side, it is whole again. Some souls find themselves in a hospital-like setting on the other side of life (in Heaven). This 'hospital' is watched over by angels in the afterlife. Occasionally, relatives on this side of life are able to witness their loved ones by being invited to visit Heaven during dream-like experiences. Sometimes, people who are unconscious as a result of an accident might get the opportunity of viewing these realms before being returned to their physical body.

Some souls 'wake up' in a heavenly hospital bed and others choose to go to healing cubicles where their souls are healed and made whole once again. Angels watch over and care for the soul while this takes place.

TRUE LIFE STORY:
MY SON VISITS HEAVEN

My mother passed away in 2005 yet my son Toby often speaks of seeing Nanny in 'the light'. When he visits her, he sees a pure white light around her and anyone else who is with her. Often these experiences are at night. His most recent visit was just a couple of nights ago. There are two things of significance to point out. The day before, Alan, a dear and close friend of our family, passed away with cancer. Secondly, Toby broke his arm two weeks ago and it is now in a plaster cast.

Toby told me, very matter-of-factly, 'Oh Mum, I forgot to tell you I saw Nanny again last night.' 'How lovely,' I replied, 'what happened?' Toby told me he was in bed and that, although he thinks he may have been asleep, he wasn't dreaming. He saw 'the light' and it went to Nanny's house. I was fascinated by what he was telling me and it seemed clear he was visiting on 'the other side', in their realms.

'Nanny asked me how I broke my arm.' Toby explained that he thought it was strange at the time because his arm was not in plaster in Nanny's 'house' (in the dream visit).

Now here is another weird thing. Toby told me: 'Oh and, Mum, I also saw Alan. He was in a bed and I was told it's because he's only just passed over and needs to rest for a while.' Toby seemed surprised when he remembered another little detail. 'Alan didn't have wrinkles any more ... his face was smooth!'

Then Toby went on to explain something he'd seen which he called 'a portal'. A small black hole was behind him to the left. He said he heard a voice directing him towards the portal because it was now time to go back. He said he ran towards it and as he was getting closer he could see his bedroom through it. Then he jumped through the hole, and found himself back in bed. He said that the first thing he did when he returned to his bedroom was hold up his arm to see if it was still in plaster. (It was.) After telling me the story, Toby was insistent on looking up the word 'portal' on the internet to try to show me an image of what he'd seen. After a few minutes on the computer he called me excitedly to say he'd found a picture of the kind of thing he experienced.

Take comfort in the fact that many souls find themselves immediately healed once they travel down the tunnel and through the light into Heaven-side. Missing limbs on Earth-side are miraculously restored on Heaven-side; people who needed wheelchairs and walking sticks in their physical life won't need these earthly contraptions in Heaven. The angels will escort souls to where they need to be in order to become whole once more.

I wouldn't tell you this if I didn't have lots of proof. Many souls come back to tell their earthly loved ones 'what happened next' on their soul's journey, and I've read numerous examples over the years.

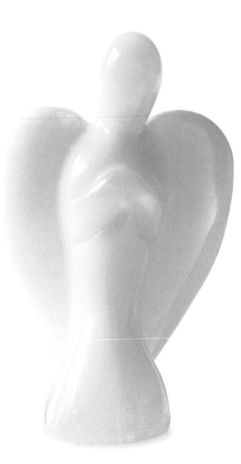

RECEIVING A VISIT FROM THE AFTERLIFE

Not many people get the opportunity of visiting the afterlife, but there are plenty of cases where the opposite happens, and spirits are happy to visit us on this side of life.

Deceased loved ones are escorted on a short trip back to the earthly realms by an angel.

To visit 'our side' of life, our angels and deceased loved ones need to alter their frequency (or the speed of their energy). This takes great effort so can only be managed for the briefest of moments.

Have you ever had a visit from a loved one with their angel from the other side of life? It's surprisingly common. Usually the angel stands in the background. Their appearance may be of a human man or woman or a tall, majestic, glowing being with wings, in true angelic form.

Sometimes the angel will announce the visit in advance, which helps to bring about a feeling of peace and calm so we are not frightened by the encounter.

Afterwards, much emotional healing takes place as we become fully aware of the reality of an afterlife. Losing a loved one can cause horrific grief, and the angels help to ease the pain by escorting our loved ones to visit us one last time.

These visits can depend on many things and, although they are common, not everyone is lucky enough to receive a visit of this sort. There are many factors that we still don't understand and these dictate whether (or if) a spirit is able to visit the earthly side of life again once their time is up. Do be comforted by the many books that have been written on the subject. There are thousands of accounts of spirits surviving physical death. Life continues on the other side.

*'I see myself in perfect health.
I am fit and well, glowing with vitality'*

ANGELS AND MONEY

'I bring you all the abundance of the Universe ... whatever you need is yours'

We are moving into a time in our history where psychic powers, which once lay dormant, will become manifest. The angels are at the forefront of this change in human evolution. Humankind has been given the gift of power over our own destiny.

For many years we have been asleep to the endless possibilities of creating our own lifestyle. Now at last the public are awakening to their powers and the angels are rejoicing. Power to manifest is not about having power over other people and forcing them to bend to your will. It's about becoming aware that your situation is very often of your own making.

For too many years people have blamed the government, their religion and their employers for the challenges they currently face in their lives. The total sum of who we are is not created out of what happened to us in the past. Our past challenges are experiences in the wheel of life from which we can learn and grow.

During my workshops I often do the 'meet your guardian angel' meditation. Often the angel hands over a gift, and you would be amazed at how many times folk receive a book with no writing on the pages, or a blank scroll. The message is: 'Create your own life, write your own play!'

As always, the angels are on hand whilst we take our first tentative steps. Change your financial situation today; plan the life you want and then begin to live it. Your new life may mean more money, but it may also mean that you earn your living in a new way. Perhaps you could create a simpler life that requires less time to be spent maintaining it financially. Think about it, then ask your angels to help you get to where you need to be.

HOW THE ANGELS HELP WITH MONEY

Most people think that angels don't work with money, but they do. Money is just another creative force in the Universe, another type of energy. In the past we used bartering to get the things we wanted; we exchanged the things we had plenty of for the objects we needed.

However, if you needed jam and the person who had the jam wanted a scarf and you had no wool to knit it with, you had to find someone with the wool who also wanted some of your home-grown carrots to exchange it for ... phew! See how exhausting this system is? It was a good idea but it had its faults.

All sorts of things have been used as money in the past, including jewellery, shells and even tea. Blocks of tea were used instead of cash in Siberia until the nineteenth century.

ANGELIC AID

Money is the modern way in which we exchange services, and angels can help when we have enough of what we need. Angels don't usually work with cash directly (although they might arrange for you to find a few coins on the floor). Angels prefer to lead us to the help we need to generate the money that is necessary to run our lives. Modern lives need money to pay for housing, heating, clothing, food and transport.

When situations are such that it's not possible to help bring the money we need into our lives, the angels help bring about the changes necessary to ensure we no longer need the money. Complicated? Yes! For example, if you're walking down the wrong path, not following your dreams, the angels might bring about a redundancy in your current work position (knowing that you have asked for these changes to come into your life so that you can follow your life plan and not become stagnant). The company you work for might therefore decide that your position is no longer required.

In a panic, your first thought is that the angels have abandoned you – but maybe the most appropriate thing for you and your family is to move away from the big old house you can no longer afford and buy a cheaper modern house (which is easier to clean and care for) and move finally to your dream location by the sea. Because your job is no longer holding you back, you can now be wherever you want to be!

EMBRACING CHANGE

Changes can be frightening, but we must see them as opportunities. Ask yourself 'What can I learn from this?' 'How can I make this work for me?'

Angels help us with what we need, and not necessarily with what we want, and it is important to remember that. With this in mind, it is often easier to accept the changes that take place in your life.

ANGEL SECRET

To generate wealth (of all kinds) you need to create a space to let it in. Ask the angels to help you make room. Do this physically to bring about the best change in your life. Empty rubbish from cupboards, give items to charity, sell old objects you no longer need (which immediately brings you money to buy the things you do need). Create space by moving on unwanted items – the space will soon be filled with what you need in your life right now.

ARCHANGELS WHO WORK WITH MONEY

The Archangels Chamuel and Michael help find lost items (money included). Michael, as the warrior angel (the angel bouncer/guard) will help to protect your money and precious items. Michael is the one to talk to if you have financial problems, although money issues are not the angels' most favoured topic – they prefer to work with love!

ASKING FOR MONEY

You can ask your angels directly for money, but it might not appear in the way you expect. Use the following to make your request. Say: Beloved angels, please help me to manifest ... (insert exact amount here) into my life in whatever ways known or unknown are most appropriate and for the highest good of all. With your will be it. (You can say 'Amen' or finish off in another way that might be appropriate to your religion if you have one, or just say 'With love and thanks'.)

If you prefer, write these words down rather than say them. Your angel might wish to bring the exact item you need rather than the cash for it. On the other hand, you might find a cheque for a tax rebate, an unexpected inheritance, interest on money in a bank account you had forgotten, or maybe just cash tucked down the arms of the sofa! The next story explains the angel solution exactly. This lady didn't suddenly find a wad of cash but she was given the help she needed – wasn't this a better solution to the problem?

ANGEL SECRET

Angels can watch over money as well as people, if you ask them. Place an angel coin (available from gift shops) or an angel picture (draw or paint something and stick it on to a small piece of card) in your purse or wallet alongside your money. Ask that the coin or picture be dedicated to this specific task. Don't forget to say 'thank you' once you have asked. Say the following words: 'Angels, I dedicate this coin/ picture as a guardian of my money ... please keep it safe.'

TRUE LIFE STORY:
NO MONEY BUT I FOUND AN ANGEL

I was 23 and pregnant with my fourth child. I was married to a brute – a very jealous and possessive man. He used to be so controlling that I was timed in whatever I did: timed at how long I spent in the WC, timed at how long I was out on the school run and timed at how long I was out shopping.

It was a bitterly cold day and the snow was deep. I had trudged the mile to the shops with my three-year-old son in the buggy and my two older girls holding on to each side. Having bought the groceries, I began the trudge back, being constantly aware of how long I was taking. I had carrier bags of shopping looped over the buggy handles and also on both of my arms. My little ones were crying with the cold.

Then about three-quarters of a mile from home, the unthinkable happened. The buggy broke. My son was screaming, my girls were crying and I just stood on the corner ankle-deep in snow and despaired at how I might get the shopping and the kids home, not to mention the trouble I would be in for getting home late. I had no money for the phone box, and mobile phones weren't common in those days. I felt utterly defeated.

Out of nowhere, a woman in a van stopped and got out. She offered to take me home! She helped load the children and shopping into the van. I knew I would be in trouble for accepting a lift as my husband didn't like me talking to people outside the home, but I figured it was worth it to get my little ones out of the cold.

The lady dropped me off right outside my door and helped me unload the kids and shopping.

Almost as soon as the last bag was out of the van, she and the van vanished! I didn't see her get back in the van, or drive away. I didn't even get into trouble for being late that day. My husband had fallen asleep, so I realized that there is a God and there are angels; I just know it!

ABUNDANCE CRYSTALS

Angels are happy to work with nature's energy enhancers. There are several crystals that relate to money. Carry one in your pocket or your handbag, or wear it in jewellery. Try working with some of the abundance crystals mentioned in the box below and see how they perform for you.

Green crystals are often used to attract wealth. Look out for angel-shaped crystals (sold by many internet stores). Some are small enough to carry around with you and others are perfect for your abundance altar.

But there is more to money than simply increasing it. You can use crystals to protect the money that you already have, or to bring more luck into your life.

ANGEL SECRET

Angels often leave little gifts for human souls. These gifts are usually small or simple like feathers and coins – pennies from Heaven. Why not ask your angel to leave you some pennies too?

Crystal	Qualities and uses
Smoky quartz	A power stone that enhances what you already have
Sapphire	Encourages more money
Clear quartz	Keep next to or on top of money to help it grow
Citrine	Protection – keeps your money safe
Aventurine	Helps you become more lucky

EXERCISE: Create an abundance altar

Once you have made an altar, you can keep it in the same place for as long as you like. Always keep your displays clean, dust-free and with fresh flowers (if you use them). Dead flowers and dusty displays will end up in exactly the same state as your empty wallet!

1 Put a small gold- or silver-painted shelf up on the wall in your home; if you prefer, you can use a small table with a gold or silver cloth or shawl over the top.

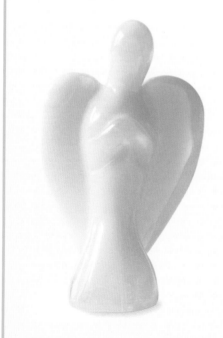

2 Place a largish angel figurine right in the centre of your display area, and next to this a gold or silver candle. The figurine represents your guardian angel, whom you ask to provide opportunities to increase your wealth.

3 To the right of the display, place a vase of fresh, yellow flowers. These will help keep the energy around your request fresh.

4 Place a chunk of rock crystal (clear quartz) on the left of the display and, underneath that, a banknote. The crystal will charge the note (like a battery).

5 Light the candle and say the following three times (a magical number):

Angels help to guide me

With abundance to provide me

6 Light the candle every time you need an extra boost of cash. Always remember to blow it out again.

ABUNDANCE AFFIRMATION

Affirmations are powerful tools for transformation or change. They are simple words and phrases formed into powerful messages that you repeat or read over and over again. Here is a money affirmation for you. Write it down or print it out and keep it by your bed. Read it through every night before you go to sleep.

Say: *I have more money than I ever dreamt possible, all the money I'll ever need with plenty left over to help many others. Thank you, angels, for my wealth.*

STRANGE BUT TRUE: MONEY STORIES

Here are a number of strange but true stories about money. Were the angels at work in any of the following experiences, do you think?

- An absent-minded passenger left a case full of cash on a bus in San Juan, Argentina. Bus driver Alberto Rios found over one and a half million pesos at the end of his shift. Alberto found the owner of the cash later looking worried and confused at a bus stop. He returned the whole case with all the money intact, leaving one to wonder why the money wasn't stolen by other passengers in the mean time. Maybe a guardian angel was really watching over the cash to prevent this from happening!

- Shunda Palmer, from Georgia, USA, had the weirdest dreams. She dreamt about a list of numbers, which she then remembered upon waking. Taking a chance, she decided to use the numbers as her choice on the next lottery draw and won over $93,000 on her lucky dream numbers!

- A student in Australia was worried about her parents' finances. Searching through a pile of old lottery tickets she found in a drawer, she was stunned to discover she had won $13 million Australian dollars on the draw. The ticket was literally just under 12 months old and due to expire in a few weeks' time. Strangely enough, the lottery ticket had been a gift from her father and the student was excited to know that she would now be able to help her parents with their financial problems.

Guardian angels intervening, or strange but true coincidences?

You decide!

BE A MONEY ANGEL: GIVE MONEY AWAY

Working with the angels to create wealth is not just about greed and self-indulgence. Money needs to flow in and out to help it to regenerate. If you want more money in your life, why not help others to create the wealth they need? Are there charities in your local community that could do with your help? Can you help to sponsor a child abroad? Find ways in which you can help bring more abundance into other people's lives.

How about tithing? Many successful people tithe (give away) 10 per cent of the money they earn. Traditionally, tithed money would go to support a religious organization or a charity in a freewill offering, intended to bring joy into your life. Some people believe that 10 per cent of your money automatically belongs to God anyway, and that you shouldn't consider it to be your money. The word tithe literally means 'tenth', but some say that originally this wasn't related to money but rather to land or other possessions.

'I am financially strong and cared for at all times'

ANGELS AND PROTECTION

*'God asks his angels to
watch over humankind.
We are with you, protecting
you and taking care of you,
our special children'*

The angel's greatest role is one of protection and some of the most magical stories I receive are those where the angels have intervened in some tragedy. Although many of life's challenges are presented to us as ways for the human soul to learn and grow, some things are not. The angels even save lives when it's 'not our time to go'. Angels perform dramatic rescues and suggest subtle changes in our plans, maybe saving our souls many times.

Have you ever planned a journey and felt a strong instinct to take a different path? Have you started to walk to a usual destination and then changed your mind for no apparent reason? Have you telephoned a friend out of the blue only to have that friend appear in desperate need of your time? The angels work with humankind to create protection coincidences – delicate little signs that guide us to help protect ourselves and others.

Our guardian angels are working behind the scenes every day. They love us, care for us and protect us. They help us find our way in the confusion that is life. By its very nature, this chapter is full of angel stories. Angel protection is our guardians' greatest gift to humankind.

GUT INSTINCT OR INTUITION

What one person calls 'gut instinct' (that feeling or knowing in the pit of your stomach) another person will call intuition or sixth sense. These feelings are your angels' way of passing a message to you. You literally 'feel' the message even though it might be difficult to explain to others what you felt.

Some people believe that these feelings are a natural way for our bodies to pick up information that keeps us safe. Wild animals live their lives like this, relying on their instincts. Have you ever had something similar happen to you? Watch out for your own inner guidance system going to work, and pay attention to the warning signals. Is your angel trying to help you? Look for the protection signs.

TRUE LIFE STORY:
AN ANGEL TO WATCH OVER YOU

I recently went to Cuba with a friend and took one of your angel books with me. My friend doesn't believe in the afterlife or angels and was laughing at how interested I was in the book.

My friend decided to do a skydive during the holiday. I was worried in case anything went wrong, so I asked the angels to protect her. Her group was landing on the beach. I prayed to the angels again and again, saying 'Please take care of my friend'. When I saw her land, I ran to give her a hug. She said: 'The instructor I was strapped to is called Gabriel.' I told her right away 'That's the name of the archangel ... and it's because I asked the angels to look after you.' My friend still wasn't sure.

The next day, she received her skydiving video. We watched it in the hotel and as the credits rolled each instructor was named. We noticed that Gabriel's name wasn't included. I knew my prayers had worked!

EXERCISE: Protect me meditation

I talked earlier in this chapter about asking your angel to protect and watch over you. This meditation will help you to do this in a formal way.

1 As usual, find a safe, warm and comfortable place to sit, perhaps an armchair in your living room. Close your eyes and relax and perform the relaxation exercise if you wish (see page 17). A warm room will help you to relax more quickly.

2 Take two or three deep, relaxing and cleansing breaths. Breathe in through your nose and blow out through your mouth ... in ... and out.

3 Now imagine you are floating gently through a rainbow of light. Like a rainbow arc, you start at the beginning, moving up and floating all the way to the other side of the rainbow. Take your time and feel the colours filtering through your body. As you move through the different colours of light, your body can absorb any colours that need topping up in your own aura.

All the while you feel relaxed and safe.

4 At the end of the rainbow is your guardian angel, waiting to catch you like a parent at the end of a fairground ride. Your angel is strong and tall. Now your angel whispers words to you: 'I am always here to catch you if you fall, to hold your hand when you're alone, to stand beside you when you're afraid ... do you give permission?' Answer 'Yes' at this point.

5 Your angel smiles in recognition at your answer. Know your angel is at your side. Know that your angel will bring you warnings and signs to keep you out of trouble – remember this is a joint operation. You and your angels work together.

6 When you're ready, open your eyes and bring your mind back into the room.

As with all other meditations, write down any thoughts or feelings you experience in your angel journal. Draw any pictures that come to mind.

ANGELS AND CHILDREN

Angels watch over children as they do adults, and children seem more likely than adults to see and experience their angel helpers. Very young children will point and smile at things unseen by the adult eye. Youngsters assume that their parents and older relatives can see the vision too.

Children's angel friends can appear as adult spirits (guides and guardians), visions in white or glowing light, or as child spirits. The 'imaginary' friend they've been talking to all week may well be a real being, perhaps a spirit guide or friend of some sort.

PROTECTION FOR CHILDREN

Why not have an angel class at home? Teach your children about angels. Knowing that an angel is watching over them can be helpful in making your child feel more secure in new and challenging situations. Here are some things to try:

• Draw a simple angel outline and ask your children to colour it in.

• Ask your child to draw an angel. What do they think an angel might look like?

• Create an angel dressing-up box. Sparkly clothes in white, silver and gold are fun. Use lengths of fabric from discount stores, old evening clothes and Christmas tree tinsel (make sure it's age-appropriate), and make a wand out of an old wooden spoon covered in silver foil. Look out for old net curtains which can be used in many ways. Many stores sell angel wings and accessories cheaply these days. Bring a little magic into your child's life.

• Perform an angel protection ritual with your child. Ask them to write down their worries and give them to the angels. If you write your message on a small piece of rice paper it can be safely thrown into water and taken away by the sea or a stream (providing food for birds).

• Children who are scared to sleep at night may well be comforted by angels. Add an angel poster or picture to the bedroom wall and explain how the angels watch over them and keep them safe at night.

*'The angels always keep me
safe and protected'*

ANGELS AND DIVINATION

'We connect with you using the magic of the divine Universe'

Picking up on your angel's subtle signs is not always easy. Angel divination, using special cards, is the perfect way of bridging the gap between intuition and direct communication. Divination is just another way of saying divining or seeing into the future or fortune-telling, although really what we are doing with the cards is using them for inspiration and guidance. They help us tune into our own intuitive thoughts. All sorts of magical experiences can happen when you read angel cards.

PACKS OF CARDS

Although they might look similar at first, angel divination cards are nothing like tarot cards (which require a great deal of study before use). Cards used for angel readings are usually fairly self-explanatory and are very easy for a beginner to start using almost immediately.

Cards usually come in a pack consisting of 40-plus assorted cards. They are typically the size of playing cards and can be shuffled and cut in the same way. Each card has a different word or phrase, consisting of positive affirmations and simple guiding thoughts. Their messages are gentle and safe, and even children enjoy picking a message from the angels. Angel inspiration cards might use words such as love or understanding, or simple phrases like 'Your angels are with you as you work' or 'Work in nature today'.

Packs can be bought from New Age stores and over the internet. There's a wide variety to choose from, and many are beautifully decorated with angel and spiritual images. They are a pleasure to use and collect (I have 30 or so different types). Most packs contain a booklet or leaflet with instructions on how to use them, but there are no rules, only guidelines. In time, you will find your own way.

BUYING DIVINATION CARDS

Choosing your cards can be a lot of fun. You might want to buy a single pack at first, but you can easily work with several packs at once if your budget allows. Unlike tarot cards, which are traditionally given as a gift, it is perfectly OK for you to choose your own angel divination cards.

Use your instincts to pick a pack of cards that feels right to you. If you can, try to buy your cards in person so that you can sense the pack. Hold your hands over each pack in turn. How does it feel? Sometimes a pack will almost call out to you. Do you experience any pull towards any particular pack? Another way to choose your cards is to try out several different packs. Good stores will have open packs that you can shuffle through, or maybe a friend has some cards you could try out. Ask your angels a question (in your head if you're shy) and pick a card from each pack in turn. Which pack gives the best answer?

Buying your cards from the internet is fine too. Try to look at as many different types of cards as possible. Some websites will even show you the inside of the pack. Print off a few pictures from each pack, and cut them out; then try the same exercise as above, holding your hand over each image in turn to see if you pick up any special vibrations that will help you choose. Some people pick cards from the images alone, and if the pictures are important to you then do that. Make notes of any thoughts and feelings about your experience in your journal.

EXERCISE: Make your own cards

You don't have to buy your angel divination cards, you can make your own – and have fun doing so. You can use the backs of old birthday or Christmas cards, or buy some pre-cut business cards from your local stationery store.

You will need some felt-tip pens and a collection of images (cut out from magazines or wrapping paper, or printed using your computer).

1 Write a list of 40 positive words, phrases or short sentences, remembering the sort of things that your angels might do to inspire you. These are the messages that will be written on each card. This will take some time, so you may want to collect your messages over several days or weeks, or ask a friend to help you.

Here are a few ideas to get you started:

• Your guardian angel protects you whilst you sleep

• Creativity and expression

• Laughter and play

• The angels are encouraging you in your latest projects

• The angels are bringing animal friends into your life

• Love and light

• Safe and secure

• Study and learning

• Ask the angels to help you with your daily tasks

• Know that your angels are protecting your loved ones

2 When the list is complete, write your messages on your cards with the felt-tip pens, leaving space for decoration. Then decorate the cards in a way that pleases you, using the images you have collected. Take your time over this. It doesn't matter if it takes several weeks; it will be worth the effort. Cards you have created yourself will always be special because they will have your own creative energy imprinted on them. Remember to jot down any notes or inspirations that you receive as you make your cards.

USING SINGLE CARDS

You can have a collection of smaller cards, which can be picked singly from a pretty glass bowl, china dish, basket or opened box. Children, in particular, love to dip into the angel cards and pick themselves an angel message. Even people who have no real interest in angels will be tempted to say 'What messages are the angels bringing me today?' Encourage them to try it for themselves.

Using single cards is a way of getting all the family involved in angel magic, and a lovely icebreaker when you have guests – just simply leave the cards on the table or pick one yourself. I bet your guests will ask to have a go!

There are several ways of using singles cards. One of the most popular is to ask a question and then pick a single card (or two, three or as many as you like) to bring you your answer. Another way of using the cards is simply to pick a single card as your inspiration for the day.

ANGEL SECRET

Angel cards are a wonderful ice-breaker. When friends come over for a meal they make the perfect entertainment.

You can pop your question again, after having given your angels and guides a little notice. Did you notice any difference between your two readings? Make a note of your answers in your angel journal.

SHUFFLING AND CUTTING THE PACK

Larger cards can be sorted using the traditional methods of shuffling or cutting the pack. Use the method above to ask the angels question, or just pick a single card or several cards for inspiration for the day ahead.

HAVE CARDS WILL TRAVEL

Angel cards are very easy to transport and there is no reason why you shouldn't be able to carry a pack around with you wherever you go.

If you wish, you could create your own mini-sized angel packaging for easy transportation. Pop the cards in a drawstring bag and include a silky (or sparkly) scarf to lay your cards on when you want to use them. Perhaps add a couple of tumbled crystals to place around the edge.

How about a mini carved crystal angel figurine too? (You can find these in gift shops, New Age stores, psychic fairs and on the internet.)

SETTING THE SCENE

If you walk around any psychic fair, you will find that each card reader has his or her own method of cleansing or preparing their cards for readings. These are a number of things that they might do.

They might:

• Pray, while holding the cards.

• Pull the cards through smoke, using an incense stick or smudge stick

• Say special words or phrases to invite the angels to assist them during their reading.

• Place crystals on or around their divination cards.

• Imagine or hold magical symbols over the cards. People who work with Reiki healing energy might use their Reiki symbols over the cards.

CREATE YOUR OWN READING TABLE

As with preparing the cards, each reader or psychic will also have their own personality stamped on their reading table. Decorating a table on which to read your cards can be lots of fun. Some of the things on your table might be practical but others will be objects that you just enjoy and like to have around you. Here are some ideas:

• Natural objects, such as flowers, stones and shells, that you have collected yourself.

• Something scented, like essential oils or natural potpourri.

• An angel figurine.

ANGEL SECRET

Always give your angels a few seconds' notice before pulling an angel card – the answers will be more accurate.

- A candle that you can light to open up your reading session and blow out at the end (make sure this is safely out of the way of your other objects – you might find it is easier to work with a candle in a glass or perhaps a tea-light in a pretty ceramic holder).

- A pretty cloth to lay on the table.

- Crystals. You could place a bowl of different-coloured tumbled crystals on the table, or perhaps some larger ones (clear quartz clusters are particularly suitable, as are rose quartz and amethyst).

- Your card box or bag.

Remember that this is your table, so anything that you love is perfect.

PROTECTING YOUR CARDS

In times gone by, all cards used for divination purposes were considered magical. They were usually protected and wrapped in either black silk or black velvet and/or placed in a wooden box. There's no need to go to such lengths to secure your cards, but you might want to make or buy something special to keep them in.

Many shops sell simple drawstring bags in pretty fabrics; or find yourself a silky scarf or old-fashioned lace handkerchief to wrap your cards in,

---

TRUE LIFE STORY:
ANGEL CARD MAGIC!

I'd been giving angel card readings all day with my angel cards and was now feeling poorly and tired. I decided to try to relax for a while and sat in my angel room and meditated, asking the angels to help heal me. I believe in angels because I work with them all the time, but like most people I still like a little proof that they are around, so I asked them if they would leave me a sign. Afterwards I went to bed. I'd left my angel cards piled up together on the table with a crystal on top as I usually do. I woke up in the early hours of the morning (about 4.30 a.m.) and hadn't slept well. I went straight into my angel room to pick up my cards. I was stunned as they had been laid out in a circle on the table. I knew I'd had my sign!

---

adapting the traditional method. Or you could buy or make yourself a fabric-covered box. Old shoeboxes are perfect for storing your angel items. Look for angel wrapping paper, attractive wallpaper or images cut from magazines – anything that inspires you – to decorate your box.

CREATE A RITUAL FOR YOUR CARDS

What sort of ritual would you like to perform before using your own cards? Would you light a candle or play special music? Would it be important for you to place certain crystals, stones, shells or other magical objects on or around your cards? Make a list of any items you would like to use as part of your angel card reading process.

Create your own special phrase to invite the angels to work with you – and don't forget to thank the angels after your reading. Here's an example:

Angel, I thank you for joining me as I use my angel cards to gather insights about my life. I would now like to open my angel card reading session.

A closing ritual might include the following (adapt it as you wish):

Angel, I thank you for your assistance and insights while using my angel cards. I would now like to close my angel card reading session.

Write all your information in a notebook or workbook so that you can refer to it again and again.

READING THE CARDS

Reading the cards is more about intuition than learning the meanings from a book. Remember that in the case of every book of 'instructions' somebody, somewhere, made it up! I want you to make up your own reading using your natural instinct and intuition.

Psychics use cards, crystal balls, rune stones and any number of different tools, but they don't have to. In time, you too will be happy to work without a tool, but while you are learning the cards will be more fun. When you draw a card from the pack, your first instinct as to the meaning of the card is nearly always the correct one. Your first thought is usually your psychic voice and your second thought is probably your logical mind jumping in.

Try this. Shuffle the pack in the normal way and pick a single card.

Read out the message on the card first of all, and write it down. What other thoughts come to mind? Write them down too. Then look at the image on the card. Does another thought or idea come to you that might be connected to the picture on the card itself ? Jot that down too.

Remember that the cards are just a tool, so while you pick a card your message might come to you in your head. In fact, it's quite possible that once you open yourself up to angelic inspiration you don't even have to look at the card to get the message.

Try this. Shuffle your pack of cards and then lay them out in front of you, face down. Pick out several cards and then give a friend an angel card reading, telling him or her what you feel the cards mean. However, and this is the fun bit, keep the cards face down and don't turn them over until the reading has been completed. Don't look at the front of the cards with the meanings at all until this time (or ever).

Write down your reading (or ask your friend to). Don't try to understand what the message means – this is not your job. Just pass on what you feel, see and sense in relation to the cards. Your message might have meaning in the future (a prediction), or maybe your friend won't understand the meaning of the reading because the circumstances won't all come together until later in the day.

If you want to, you can check the messages on the front of the cards afterwards and compare your original reading with the actual messages. Just remember, though, that you are using the cards as a tool only – a tool to open up your natural psychic and angelic awareness.

CREATING A 'SPREAD'

A 'spread' is a traditional way of reading divination cards. It sounds complicated, but it needn't be. A spread is simply a pattern of cards in which the reader has decided the general meaning or purpose of each card in advance. The pattern of cards can be as simple or as complicated as you wish.

Simple spreads

For example, you could pick four cards and lay them face down in a square. You may decide that the top right-hand card is related to money, the top left-hand card is related to family, the bottom right-hand card is about love and the final card is the one you are going to read in respect of your career.

Then turn over each card in turn. What message is on the front of your angel card? How might the message relate to your love interest, family, money or career (depending on the position of the card)?

In your notebook, draw out some card patterns or spreads (in lines, cross shapes, circles or any shape you want). Give each card an advance meaning, then name your spread – for example, 'Circle of life' for a circle of cards). This is your reading, so you decide on its name.

Spread suggestions

Play around with your spreads and practise your new readings on friends – trust me, they will love it. Here are two I use myself. Three-card 'past, present, future' spread Shuffle or cut the pack, then pick three cards. Place them face down in a line going away from you. The furthest card away from you represents the past, the card nearest to you the future, and the card in the middle the present, as laid out below:

PAST (furthest away)

PRESENT (middle)

FUTURE (closest)

Turn over each of your cards one at a time, starting with the card that represents your past. What does the card have to say about your past? Then turn over your present card. How does the card relate to your present? Last of all, turn over the card that represents your future.

ANGEL SECRET

Make a teeny set of angel cards out of small pieces of card (just one word on each), then carry them in your bag or pocket so you always have some angel assistance when you need it.

What inspirational thoughts come to mind with your future card?

Four-card 'life' spread

Shuffle or cut the pack and place four cards face down in a square (two rows of two cards). As before, each card represents a different area of your life. In this case the cards represent your love life, your career, your finances and your creativity. Lay them out like this:

LOVE LIFE (top left)

CAREER (top right)

FINANCES (bottom left)

CREATIVITY (bottom right)

Turn over each of your cards one at a time (the reading order is up to you but it is usual to read the cards either clockwise (top left, top right, bottom right and then bottom left) or left to right, one row at a time (in the same way you would read a book) – in this case: Love life, Career, Finances, Creativity As before, though, I want you to use your cards in the way that feels right to you.

Remember, as well as taking note of the actual message on the card, to use your judgement by looking at the picture on the card and recording, in your angel journal, any immediate thoughts or images that come to mind as you turn it over.

MAKE UP YOUR OWN SPREADS

You can, of course, make up your own spreads using any formula or pattern you wish. Try lining up several cards in each column to give you more than one card relating to each subject or query. Or combine the two spreads suggested above to do a past, present and future spread relating to your love life, your career, your finances and your creativity.

Other areas to question might include:

• travel

• health

• wealth

• family

• study

• future directional advice

• pets

• home

• friends

Remember the reading is about you and your choices rather than you asking the angels to bring you personal and private information about others.

THE POWER OF PRACTICE

Practise as much as you can. The more you use your cards, the more comfortable you will become. Don't just stick to one pack; there is no reason why you can't use two packs together or do two different readings for yourself using one pack for one reading and one for the other. If you are using a bought pack of cards, it is not necessary to use the instruction booklet. In fact, I suggest that you don't even read it until you are comfortable with using the cards in your own way. Later on, you might want to check out the book to give you further ideas and suggestions. Do remember that there is no right or wrong way of using the cards – only your way. Feel empowered and take control!

TRUE LIFE STORY:
SPECIAL ANGEL READINGS

I've never had any training on how to read the angel cards and just picked it up as I went along. When I did a psychic reading, I used to read without cards and just deal four angel cards face down as I was speaking. When I turned them over they exactly repeated the reading ... every time!

READING FOR OTHERS

Once you feel comfortable reading your angel cards for yourself, you will be ready to practise on others. I promise that you will have plenty of willing volunteers! Tell your friends that the reading is for fun only. Confidence is everything if you want to appear the 'expert' that you have now become.

Reading for others is very different to reading for yourself, and there are a few simple rules of etiquette:

DOS

• Remember that a reading consists of your own personal thoughts and inspirations surrounding the chosen cards, so you should begin with 'I feel that ... (your message)' or 'This card means ... (your message) to me'.

• Remember that a card reading is one interpretation of a past, present or future. Your 'client' therefore has control of their own choices in this area. There is a universal thought that we create our own reality. Share this thought with your 'client' so that you may empower them rather than make them dependent on you and your readings to decide their life path. Even better, teach your friend how to use the cards to create their own readings.

DONT'S

• Never promise to predict someone's future. Remember that a 'prediction' is only the most likely outcome based on the current set of circumstances, and we can change this at any time.

• Never tell anyone anything negative in your reading. Angel cards are positive, inspirational messages and you should stick to the spirit of the angel card reading and pass on your insights in this way.

• Don't fall into the trap of thinking that angels tell us what to do; they can only support our choices or guide us in making decisions for ourselves. So we must not tell people what to do either.

EXERCISE: Do a reading for a friend

OK, now for the fun bit. If possible, lay out your reading table in the way that you planned. Decorate it so that it inspires you, remembering your cloth, figurines, crystals and so on.

1 Either shuffle your cards and then get your friend to cut the pack, or ask your friend to shuffle the pack. Some people don't like others to touch their angel cards at all and like to lay them out on the table and ask their 'client' to pick the cards by pointing to them. You decide.

2 Lay your cards out in a spread. Pick one of the methods you have learnt here or, even better, use one of your own ideas, laying the cards face down and turning them over one at a time. Share all your inspirational thoughts with your friend. You might be surprised at how accurate you can be. Your friend might like to write down their reading so that they can check up on things they don't understand.

3 When you have finished your reading, don't forget to thank your friend and thank the angels. I am sure your friend will be happy for you to practise on them again. Try to read for as many people as you can – friends, family and strangers. Often it is easier to read for people whom you don't know well.

Remember to make your own notes, keeping a record of your 'hits' and 'misses', so that you can check on your progress. Don't worry if you get things wrong. The more you practise the better you will become.

'I ask my angels to protect me, to comfort me, to watch over me at all times'

ANGELS FOR EVERY DAY

*'I am with you every day,
in every way. Ask and
I will help you'*

Angels are around us and working with us every day. There are angels for every role and angels for every task. God assigned his angels with guardianship over people, animals, bodies of water and stretches of land. As we have already seen, there are angels to help with love, healing, friendships and many other things.

KNOW YOUR ANGELS

This chapter is designed as a bit of fun to help you find angels who can work with you. Look for the angels that are relevant in your life, and call on them to help you with any challenges that you are facing. Use their names (and images of them) to illustrate your angel journal and your craft work.

Your angels are there for the simple everyday things as well as emergencies. If you're in trouble, you can just call on the relevant angel to assist you. Better still, work with more than one angel at a time – your birthday angel and a suitable angel or two from the angel emergency 'telephone book', for example.

Try working with different angels for different things. Record your experiences with each angel (write them in your journal). You will soon develop a list of favourites.

ANGEL SECRET

Your angels need your permission to protect and care for you. Ask your angels for their help when you're frightened and alone. Ask your angels to be with you.

YOUR PERSONAL ANGELS

Different angels represent days of the week and months of the year. What day of the week were you born on, in which month? Use your answers to help find out which angels are yours and call upon them when you need help from the celestial realms.

YOUR BIRTH-DAY ANGEL

If you were born on a Tuesday, your angel's strength is at its strongest on a Tuesday. If you were born on a Wednesday, call on your birth angel on a Wednesday for the best possible outcome, and so on. Ask your birth angel for protection and healing and to back up your own guardian angel.

YOUR BIRTH-MONTH ANGEL

Here are the angels who represent each day of the month. Each of them has an affirmation that will help bring certain attributes into your life. Now you have quite a collection of angel helpers to call upon every day! Make a note of yours, so that you don't forget them.

Birth-day angel	Day
Gabriel	Monday
Zamael	Tuesday
Raphael	Wednesday
Sachiel	Thursday
Anael	Friday
Cassiel	Saturday
Michael	Sunday

Birth-month angel	Month	Affirmation
Cambiel	January	I am ready to wash away the old to clear a path for new opportunities in my life.
Barchiel	February	I am open to information and views of different types, which will help me to see the clearer picture.
Malahidael	March	I am safe as I achieve my objective and help others along the way.
Asmodel	April	I am clear in where I want to go and what I want to be – I easily become these things.
Ambriel	May	I am open to advice and changes and confident in new situations.
Muriel	June	I am confident and able to protect myself in uncomfortable situations.
Verchiel	July	In every way I will use my own strengths to assist others less fortunate.
Hamaliel	August	I am self-assured. I will complete my tasks in my own quiet, comfortable way.
Zuriel	September	I live my life in perfect balance.
Barbiel	October	I know I am well taken care of and looked after.
Advachiel	November	I have everything I need to get to where I want to be.
Hanael	December	Moving forward one step at a time will enable me to reach new heights.

ZODIAC ANGELS

Each angel takes charge of a different sign of the zodiac. If you choose, you can work with your own special zodiac angel (as well as your guardian angel) and call upon them when you need help. Your zodiac angel is particularly helpful when working on aspects of your spirituality or personality that relate to your birth sign.

Aquarius The vibrational energy of the angel of Aquarius is one relating to the giving of life. The Aquarius angel symbolically washes away the old and cleans the way for a fresh new beginning. If you are born under this sign, then your angel is especially good at helping with new beginnings. Ask your angel to help you to clear a pathway through the old so that you can begin anew.

Pisces The Pisces angel can always see things from more than one perspective and will always be able to help you discover both sides of any argument. Symbolized by two fish swimming in opposite directions, your zodiac angel will help protect you from that feeling of being pulled in two directions.

Aries The angel who sits under the symbol of Aries brings power and direction to any situation. If this is your angel, then you have assistance and guidance as a strength. The Aries angel will always be there to help you complete tasks, create results and motivate others around you.

Taurus The energy of this symbol also shows strength and power but with a little more aggression than Aries, as befits the sign – this angel works with true passion! Yet the angel is dependable and single-minded, helping you to get to where you want to go, and when. The angel of Taurus will hold your hand right to the end, leading your way as much as walking beside you.

Gemini The Gemini angel has communication at its heart and brings the energy of adaptability into any situation. Your angel can help you to make changes to your agenda to better move forward, and assists in learning and studying, This angel is always looking at all the options available to you and may show you a different, more appropriate route if you ask for help.

Cancer The power of this angel is related to the protection of the sensitive among those who fall under this sign. Sometimes this sign is hurt by words more than anything else; the Cancer angel is most aware of this and will work on shielding you and making you stronger and better able to face an attack from others on your own.

Leo Your Leo angel, like the sign, shows great courage at all times. Resolutely fearless, this angel will lead you onwards in its 'royal' manner but in a humble way befitting the greatness of its role. If this is your sign, then ask that your angel shows you how to inspire greatness in others and at the same time express humility. It is not about what your angels can do for you but how they can help you to help others.

Virgo A gentle angel who works in a quiet manner, usually experienced as feminine in nature, and, like the sign, 'virginal' (representing innocence). Don't be mistaken into thinking that this sign angel is less powerful than any of the others; she just gets results in a less forceful way. Call on the Virgo angel if you want a task completed in a quiet, out-of-the-limelight way.

Libra If this is your zodiac angel, then you are working with a fair judge. Your angel always wants to keep the peace and in all cases search out ways to create harmony. If what you want is help in walking the middle ground, or finding ways of walking the centre line in any situation, you can always call on the help of the Libra angel.

Scorpio This angel has the ability to get things done 'behind the scenes'. Whatever you are doing, they are busy bringing everything together – you are the star and they are the manager. While you show the world your happy face, the Scorpio angel is doing the 'dirty work' for you (in a good way). Call on this angel to help if you need someone to watch your back now and again!

Sagittarius If you are going somewhere, take this angel with you. The angel of Sagittarius is heading straight for the top and is happy for you to tag along. This angel works with development of the inner self so if you are on a spiritual pathway then this angel can help you keep to your route.

Capricorn As the old saying goes 'slowly and surely wins the race', this is how the angel of Capricorn operates. Ever chipping away at the problem, your angel is a quiet companion always with their eye on the prize, surefooted and true – but never without a touch of humour along the way. If you need regular input from an angel who is always putting one foot in front of the other, then you should ask this angel to work with you.

EXERCISE: Angel portraits and cards

Use the information listed under the birth-day and month angels to make an angel portrait.

1 Draw or paint a picture of your day or month angel. You don't have to be talented – just ask the angels to inspire you. It doesn't matter if you can't draw faces or hands. Many angels appear as glowing figures of light, so create this.

2 Use glitter to add sparkles of light to your artwork.

3 If you draw your month angel, maybe add your zodiac symbol in the corner of your print, or stick on jewels to represent it.

4 Place the angel print in a special frame in your bedroom.

If you enjoy using the daily messages on page 168), why not make use of them as angel cards that you can carry around in your bag or pocket?

1 Write up the messages in your best handwriting on little pieces of card, or print the sentences out on a computer.

2 If you prefer to draw your angels for inspiration, make an image of the relevant day or month angel instead.

3 Decorate your cards, or even laminate them (if you have access to a laminator) to keep them looking nice.

4 Put the cards on your computer or desk, or keep them with you throughout the relevant day.

ANGEL TELEPHONE BOOK

Human beings are born with what is called 'free will'. That means that we make our own choices in life, both right and wrong. Our angels can help if we give them permission. You can also call on your own guardian angel to help you in every situation, but if you want a little extra help 'who ya gonna call?'.

HOW TO USE THE 'TELEPHONE BOOK'

Although you can simply ask for 'the right angel to help', it might be quicker to request a specific angel for the job – that is, call 'direct'. Copy out the list on these pages and keep it in your angel journal, or keep a copy to carry around in your bag. I bet there are some angels you will use again and again.

Do you keep a personal journal? Look for trends in personal problems and write in the relevant angel next to your text. If you have problems with paying a bill, call on the assistance of the angel Michael by writing his name directly on your copy of the bill. If you are starting a new job, write down the name of the angel Gabriel on the date you start. This also works with your diary or home calendar. If you need particular angels on certain days (where you have appointments that need a little extra help, write the name of the relevant angel next to

your appointment). The angel Michael might be useful for protection on a school trip, for example, or the angel Raphael next to a date with the dentist. Keep a small chalkboard or whiteboard In your kitchen. Look up the most useful angels of the day and write a list on your board – change daily or as necessary.

A
Afterlife – Azrael
Anger – Gabriel
Animals – Ariel
Arguments – Raguel/Gabriel

B
Babies – Sandalphon
Bills – Michael
Birds – Ariel
Birth – Raphael
Bodyguard – Michael

C
Car trouble – Michael
Careers – Gabriel
Children – Sandalphon
Communication – Gabriel
Confidence – Gabriel

D

Danger – Michael
Dieting – Metatron
Disagreements – Raguel/Gabriel
Disease – Raphael

E

Earth healing – Uriel
Exams – Haniel
Exhaustion – Raphael
Eyesight – Ariel

F

Faith – Sandalphon
Fire – Michael
Fish – Azrael
Friendships – Gabriel

G

Gardens – Uriel
Ghosts – Michael
Grief – Azrael
Guidance – Raziel

H

Hair – Jophiel
Healing/health – Raphael
Holidays – Raphael
Home protection – Michael
Home repairs – Chamuel
Hospitals – Raphael

I, J

Illness – Raphael
Insecurities – Raphael
Jealousy – Raphael

L

Learning – Gabriel
Legal issues – Raguel
Lost items – Chamuel
Love – Haniel

M

Making things – Jeremiel

Manifestation – Uriel
Money worries – Michael

N, O

Nature – Ariel
New job – Gabriel
Opportunities – Chamuel
Outdoor spaces – Uriel

P, Q

Pets – Ariel
Prayers – Sandalphon
Protection – Michael
Psychic development – Jeremiel
Quiet time – Metatron

R

Relationships – Metatron
Remembering – Jeremiel
Repairs – Michael
Romance – Haniel

S

Safety – Michael
Security – Michael
Sleep problems – Michael
Spiritual development – Jeremiel

T

Teeth – Raphael
Tests – Gabriel
Transport – Michael
Travel – Raphael

U, V

Understanding – Gabriel
Unknown – Raziel
Vision – Ariel

W

Wars – Chamuel
Weather – Uriel
Worrying – Gabriel
Women's issues – Sariel

ANGEL DAILY MESSAGES

What day of the week is it? Follow the guide below to inspire your day. Use the messages to set your daily goals.

Monday Today I will take the first step to become who I really want to be. With my angels by my side, I will stand tall and start taking chances. By stepping out of my comfort zone I will progress on my path. Go for it!

Tuesday Today I will begin to think positively about my life. By being grateful for the things I have, I know that the angels will help me to bring more into my life. Think positively!

Wednesday Today I shall eat the foods that bring me health and vitality. I shall be full of energy, which will enable me to fulfil any task I want with minimum effort. My angels will help me to choose the perfect food for my body. Eat well!

Thursday Today is the first day of a happy new me. My angels can help to uplift and inspire me to a life full of fun and laughter. Be happy!

Friday Today I will celebrate my life and achievements to the full. There are so many wonderful things that make up my life, and today I will look only at the good ones. With my angels at my side I can enjoy everything that is great. Celebrate your life!

Saturday Today I will help others. By performing spontaneous acts of kindness, I will become a better and more fulfilled person. My angels will guide me to help those in need. Help others!

Sunday Today I will take time to appreciate the gifts of nature. God has provided me with beautiful skies, plants, birds, fish and animals to enjoy. I will get outside, if possible, or absorb myself in the delights of nature by reading or watching programmes about our diverse and beautiful planet. Appreciate nature!

*'I live my life full of fun,
joy and laughter.'*

INDEX

ACKNOWLEDGEMENTS

Material previously published as *Angel Secrets* in 2010 by Godsfield, a division of Octopus Publishing Group Ltd

Author's acknowledgements
A big thank you to all my fans around the world. Thank you for your continued support and thank you for all your questions in letters, emails and messages on Twitter and Facebook that helped to create the inspiration behind this book. I hope you enjoy this book as much as I enjoyed creating it for you.

Publisher's acknowledgements
Thank you to the following companies and people for lending us material for photography.

Angel Silver Jewellery
www.angel-silver-jewellery.com
(angel charm bracelets and pendants)

Camel & Yak www.camelandyak.co.uk
(wooden angel wings, photo frames and wire heart frame)

Cocoa Dodo www.cocoadodo.com
(framed paper angel wings)

Cox & Cox www.coxandcox.co.uk
(wooden angel wings)

Emily Coco Christie (angel drawing)

Emma Ferguson (various angel treasures)

Fleur Bruneau-Cordell (angel drawing)

George Bassirian (angel drawing)

Grace and Favour
(beautiful gifts, jewellery, clothes)

Higher Heart www.higherheart.com
(charms, crystals, figurines, cards)

Ivy Rose Ltd www.ivy-rose.co.uk (angel pen)

Jaccylee Jewellery and Designs
www.jaccylee-jewellery.co.uk
(angel bag charms, angel phone charms and crystal pendant)

Linda Keating (charm garlands)

MacCulloch and Wallis
www.macculloch-wallis.co.uk
(haberdashers, trimmings, feathers)

Moonhelene123 (angel bead charms)

Mysteries www.mysteries.co.uk (charms, crystals, books, candles, figurines)

Paperchase www.paperchase.co.uk
(journals and cards)

Pedlars www.pedlars.co.uk
(real feather angel wings)

Re-Found Objects
www.re-foundobjects.com
(angel wings, hearts, photoframes made from recycled materials)

Rockett St George
www.rockettstgeorge.co.uk
(angel wing necklaces and bracelets)

Say It With Angels
www.sayitwithangelswholesale.com
(guardian angel box, guardian angel wing frame, angel coins and angel brooches)

Swedish Interior Design
www.swedishinteriordesign.co.uk and www.madeleinelee.co.uk (handmade angel)

Talking Beads www.talkingbeads.co.uk
(angel bookmarks and angel key rings)

The Fresh Flower Company
www.freshflower.co.uk (flowers)

Picture acknowledgements
All photography © Octopus Publishing Group/Polly Wreford; except for the feather Images on pp. 9, 20, 45, 61, 69, 77, 85, 89, 111, 117, 129, 153, and 155 © Robert Red/Shutterstock